L♦ST
IN THE PACIFIC, 1942

NOT A DROP
TO DRINK

TOD OLSON

Scholastic Inc.

For Richard and Estie,
who made sure I did not get lost

TABLE OF CONTENTS

THE CASTAWAYS

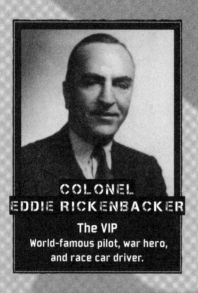

COLONEL
EDDIE RICKENBACKER

The VIP
World-famous pilot, war hero,
and race car driver.

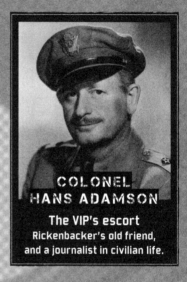

COLONEL
HANS ADAMSON

The VIP's escort
Rickenbacker's old friend,
and a journalist in civilian life.

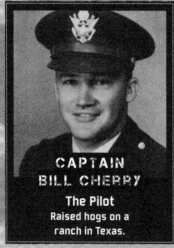

CAPTAIN
BILL CHERRY

The Pilot
Raised hogs on a
ranch in Texas.

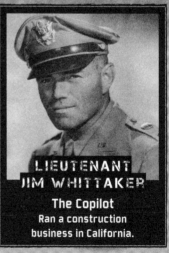

LIEUTENANT
JIM WHITTAKER

The Copilot
Ran a construction
business in California.

**LIEUTENANT
JOHN DEANGELIS**

The Navigator
Drove a truck in Pennsylvania
and loved to dance.

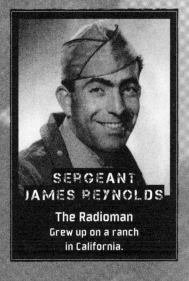

**SERGEANT
JAMES REYNOLDS**

The Radioman
Grew up on a ranch
in California.

**SERGEANT
ALEX KACZMARCZYK**

The Engineer
Loved music and worked in a
gas station in Connecticut.

**PRIVATE
JOHNNY BARTEK**

The Other Engineer
Dropped out of high school and
wanted to be a photographer.

OCTOBER 21, 1942
SOMEWHERE OVER THE SOUTH PACIFIC

The Pacific Ocean looked calm and inviting from 5,000 feet up, with the drone of four sturdy motors in Jim Whittaker's ear. But he had no desire to land a 15-ton, 4-engine plane down there. To a B-17 bomber, plunging from the sky, the ocean is as unforgiving as a concrete wall.

Yet by 1:30 p.m. on October 21, 1942, that was the only option left. Whittaker was the B-17's copilot. He and the rest of the crew were ferrying a VIP passenger on a top-secret mission deep into the war zone. They had completely missed Canton Island, the tiny speck in the great blue where they were supposed to refuel. Now they were flying in a giant square pattern, hoping to spot land. They took turns staring out the windows at the ocean below, mistaking cloud shadows for islands. "Island eyes," the airmen called it—the surest sign that desperation had set in.

The Plane: A 15-ton, 4-engine B-17.

The fact was they were lost, somewhere in the middle of the Pacific. They were nearly out of fuel, and the only landing strip they had was a vast tarmac of water.

No one knew exactly how they had lost their way. Maybe the tailwinds were stronger than the weathermen had predicted. Maybe the compass had taken a hit when they nearly crashed taking off in Hawaii. Either way, the navigator had finally given up trying to figure out where they were. He was a young guy named John DeAngelis who had gotten married just two days before they were called away. Now he was probably wondering if he would ever see his wife again.

"Do you fellows mind if I pray?" he shouted to the crew over the roar of the engines.

Pray? Whittaker thought. How about keeping your mind on the task at hand: surviving an impact with the Pacific Ocean.

Whittaker decided not to say a word. DeAngelis could swan dive into the ocean and it wouldn't matter. Their lives were in Bill Cherry's hands now—the twenty-seven-year-old pilot from Texas who sat next to Whittaker with the controls in his hands.

Cherry and Whittaker began to talk strategy. It had been ten and a half months since the United States was drawn into World War II. In that time, plenty of bomber crews had ditched in the Pacific. Not one, as far as they could remember, had escaped without casualties.

If the surface of the ocean were flat, it would be one thing. But today, the water rose and fell in treacherous swells. If you came in across the current you would have to time it exactly right. Scrape the crest of a swell and the nose would dip, sending the plane plummeting to the depths. Avoid one crest and you could ram the plane into the next one, shattering the entire craft into pieces in an instant.

There was only one way to do it, Whittaker and Cherry agreed. Come in parallel to the swells and set the plane down in a trough. That, of course, was easier said than done. The troughs were a moving target, and the wind blew across your flight path, making it hard to hold a line.

Hitting a landing spot just right would still take perfect timing, expert piloting skills, and a whole lot of luck.

While Cherry and Whittaker worked out a strategy, their top secret passenger took charge of the crew behind them. And if luck really had anything to do with their fate, maybe he would tip the scales in their favor. He wasn't some desk-bound politician or stuffy diplomat. The VIP on board was none other than Eddie Rickenbacker.

For anyone who cared about flying—and for most everyone else—that was all the introduction he needed. Aside from Charles Lindbergh, he was the world's most famous pilot. He hadn't flown in combat since 1918, when World War I ended. But to millions of Americans, his heroics against the Germans were unforgettable. He had shot down more enemy aircraft than any other American pilot.

Now Rickenbacker was a businessman—president of Eastern Air Lines. But he had a well-known reputation for surviving close scrapes. He had first become famous as an auto racer, driving primitive cars at breakneck speeds. As a fighter pilot, he nearly had his plane shredded by German bullets several times. Then, in the spring of 1941, he had been a passenger on one of his own airliners when it crashed in a Georgia forest. Trapped in the wreckage, he managed to direct rescue efforts with broken ribs, a

The Ace: Rickenbacker in France near the end of World War I.

shattered elbow, a fractured skull, and an eyeball torn loose from its socket. He was in such bad shape that the famous radio commentator Walter Winchell reported his death on the air. When Rickenbacker heard it from his hospital bed, he picked up a water pitcher and threw it at the radio.

A year and a half later, Rickenbacker still looked frail from the crash and walked with a cane. But now, with another crash looming, he seemed determined to survive one more time. Rickenbacker grabbed the young sergeant, Alex Kaczmarczyk, and pried open the bottom hatch in the B-17's tail. Then he and Kaczmarczyk lightened the plane's load to save fuel and lessen the impact when they went down. Out went the cots, tool kit, blankets, empty thermos bottles, and luggage. Sacks full of high-priority mail sailed into the wind, soon to be a soggy, unreadable mess of good wishes that would never make it to the soldiers on the front lines.

Cherry announced he was starting his descent, and the water outside Whittaker's window looked more distinct by the second. Back in the radio compartment, the men piled essential provisions by the hatch: a few bottles filled with water and coffee; emergency rations in a small metal box; a two-man raft rolled into a tight package. Once they landed, they might have as little as thirty seconds to get out before the plane went under—assuming they were still alive.

The men stacked mattresses in position, padding the aft, or rear, side of the walls that separated the compartments of the plane. They all took their positions. Three men—Kaczmarczyk, DeAngelis, and Rickenbacker's military escort, Colonel Hans Adamson—lay on the floor, braced against the mattresses. Rickenbacker sat near them, belted into a seat near a window. Johnny Bartek, the engineer, sat just behind the cockpit. The plane had two inflatable rafts packed into compartments on the outside of the nose. It would be Bartek's job to release them just after they ditched. James Reynolds, the radio operator who went by Jim, sat at his desk in the center of the plane. He tapped out SOS after SOS, hoping that someone out there would register their location before they hit the water. There was nothing but silence from the other end.

"How much longer?" someone asked.

"Not yet," Rickenbacker answered, peering out the window.

In the cockpit, the altimeter showed they were 500 feet above the sea. Cherry cut two of the engines to save fuel. Whittaker grabbed cushions from the seats behind them and stuffed them under their safety harnesses.

"It's sure been swell knowing you, Bill," he said, offering his hand.

Cherry gripped his copilot's hand for a second, and then said in his Texas drawl, "You're going to know me a long time yet, Jim."

In the back, someone asked again, "How much longer?"

"Fifty feet!" said Rickenbacker. Then, right away, "Thirty feet!"

Cherry was staring into the waves, trying to pick a trough to aim for. The swells looked towering—twice the height of a man.

"Twenty feet!"

They were coming in at 90 miles an hour, but to Whittaker the plane seemed strangely still—the roar of the engines muffled, the whoosh of the wind against the fuselage fainter than it should have been. And then there was the radio, whining its lonely signal into the sky.

"Ten feet!"

Bartek reached above them and loosened a set of bolts. The wind snatched the door of the cockpit escape hatch and sent it hurtling to the sea. A rush of air howled through the opening.

"Cut it!" yelled Cherry.

Whittaker pulled a switch, and all electrical power on the plane went dead. Cherry pulled back hard on the wheel, lifting the nose and ramming the tail into the water.

Back in the radio compartment, the noise was deafening. Pieces of equipment that had been bolted down a moment ago flew through the cabin like shrapnel from a bomb.

And then the belly of the plane hit the water.

Whittaker exploded forward, and the safety belt tried to slice him in half. Pressure filled his head. His eyes strained against their sockets. He couldn't see a thing. He began to lose consciousness.

And then, just as suddenly as it had begun, the pressure released. The belt went slack against his chest. His vision returned.

They had gone from 90 miles an hour to a dead stop in less than 50 feet. He couldn't be sure who had survived and who had not. The Pacific Ocean was pouring fast into the plane. And no one in the big, broad world knew where they were.

CHAPTER 1

TOP SECRET

J ust two days before they vanished to the world, Jim Whittaker and the four members of his regular Air Transport Command crew had been looking forward to some time off. Air Transport crews didn't fly combat missions, but they served an important purpose in a war that ranged far and wide across the globe. They flew planes, supplies, and people from training bases to the battlefront and back again. Whittaker, Cherry, DeAngelis, Bartek, and Reynolds had been doing this for ten months, since the U.S. entered the war. They had just picked up a B-24 "Liberator" bomber in the South Pacific and brought it to Hawaii. That afternoon they were scheduled to fly a B-17 from Hawaii to San Francisco. Then they'd take off for a well-earned leave.

John DeAngelis, the crew's navigator, couldn't wait to see his new bride, Mary. She was his high school sweetheart, and she had flown out from Pennsylvania to

California for the wedding. They'd been forced to cut the celebrations short when DeAngelis was called to duty to pick up the B-24.

The radioman, Jim Reynolds, had gotten engaged in between his six trips across the Pacific, so he was eager to get home, too.

Johnny Bartek, the engineer, was the youngest of them all at twenty-two. Less than a month ago, he'd opened a letter from his parents in Freehold, New Jersey. The news left him numb. Back home, his sister Ruth had hit her head on a wall while roller-skating. Blood pooled inside her brain from the impact, and the next day she died on the way to school. It was hard to get your mind around: Out in the world, men were surviving onslaughts of bullets and bombs, and his sister had died walking to school.

Ruth had been born on his birthday, August 30. She was seventeen years old. Bartek just wanted to get home to his family.

At 5 p.m. the crew strode across Hickam airfield toward their plane. The bright blue waters of Pearl Harbor glistened a few hundred yards to the west. It was so peaceful in the Hawaiian sun that Jim Whittaker had trouble imagining the violence that had torn this place apart ten months ago when the Japanese had launched a surprise attack. But this was where the war had started for all of them,

The giant battleship *Oklahoma* lies crippled in the waters of Pearl Harbor, fifteen months after the attack.

and the signs were still there. Bullet holes pockmarked the airplane hangars. A giant crane towered over the harbor, preparing to haul the crippled battleship *Oklahoma* upright again. At night, army police patrolled the streets to make sure all lights were out—in case the bombers came back.

It was just after dawn on December 7, 1941, when 353 Japanese planes came screaming out of the sky over the U.S. naval base at Pearl Harbor. People who lived near the base thought it was just another combat exercise. Their morning coffee had been interrupted before by the sound of machine-gun fire. This time, a dark cloud began to rise over the harbor, and many people thought it was a smoke screen laid down for the latest in a series of training games.

But the navy men aboard the warships in the harbor knew only too well that this was no game. The bombs fell on battleships, cruisers, and destroyers. Fuel tanks exploded into flames. A 16-inch shell tore into the battleship *Arizona*'s forward magazine, and a searing column of fire erupted thousands of feet into the air. Fragments of steel and wood rained down on the wreckage. Human body parts fell from the sky. Men who had been burned snow-white stumbled on the decks until they fell over. Before long, eighteen ships lay crippled at the surface or sank to the bottom of the harbor.

At the airfields, planes swept in so low that some people remembered making eye contact with the enemy pilots. Forty-three fighter planes—lightning-quick Japanese Zeros—hit Hickam Field right where Whittaker walked ten months later. They sprayed machine-gun fire like sheets of rain. Airmen were gunned down while they raced to

December 7, 1941: An explosion rocks the Naval Air Station at Pearl Harbor.

their planes. At Hickam alone, 189 people were killed. Of the four hundred aircraft on the island, just sixty escaped damage. Exactly eight made it into the air to fight back.

Unless you counted the American Revolution, the United States had been attacked by a foreign power only once in 166 years—in 1812. Now it had happened again.

"A date which will live in infamy," President Franklin Roosevelt proclaimed. Then he declared war on Japan. Germany rushed to the defense of its Japanese ally and declared war on the United States. The American people

Call to Arms: The day after Pearl Harbor, the U.S. was at war with Japan. Posters like this one encouraged Americans to support the fight.

suddenly found themselves swept into World War II, the most destructive war in history.

Whittaker, who had been flying single-engine planes since his twenties, put his construction business on hold and joined the army. At forty, he was too old to fly in combat, but he figured if he flew transport planes it would free up a younger pilot to fight.

———◆———

When the crew arrived at their B-17 that October afternoon and found new orders waiting for them, Whittaker took it in stride. They were headed back into the Pacific. There would be no trip home to see his wife and his sixteen-year-old daughter; no side trip to visit the navy base in San Francisco where his son was training. But this was what Jim Whittaker had signed up for.

Besides, the orders that were handed to Captain Cherry announced the name of their famous passenger: Eddie Rickenbacker. The crew talked about it on the way back to the base as they waited for their new takeoff time. If you had to lose a few days off, this wasn't a bad reason. They'd all get to meet the great flying ace. And with Rickenbacker aboard, chances were they'd get as close to the action as possible.

The crew were back at the plane well before the 10:30 p.m. takeoff time, checking instruments, stowing food, topping off the fuel tanks. They were joined by Alex Kaczmarczyk, a second engineer who was there to help Bartek keep the plane running smoothly. The B-17 wasn't exactly a luxury ride. It was a giant, clumsy fighting machine known as the "Flying Fortress." When it went to war it lived up to its name, carrying at least five machine guns and more than two tons of bombs. For transport missions, the gear was stripped out, but some things remained the same. The planes were still unheated, open to the air, and deafeningly loud.

Exactly two minutes before takeoff, Whittaker felt the plane rock under the weight of two new passengers. In a moment, the VIP came up behind him and introduced himself, only one name needed.

"My name is Rickenbacker."

He introduced his military aide, Colonel Hans Adamson. But it was clear he was in no mood for small talk. Rickenbacker and Adamson took the two seats just behind Whittaker and Cherry and belted in for takeoff.

Bartek, the engineer from New Jersey, came forward to find that Adamson had taken his seat. But Private Bartek had been in the military long enough to know how things worked. Officers got the best of everything, and privates were left to pick up the crumbs. Like a lot of enlisted men, he'd grumble about it when there was no one around who outranked him, but he wouldn't dream of arguing with a colonel. Bartek found another seat and strapped in.

With all eight men aboard, Cherry pulled onto the runway and picked up speed. They were halfway to liftoff and well above 60 miles an hour when one of the brakes suddenly seized. The plane lurched left and careened toward the hangars.

Rickenbacker started to get up. He opened his mouth to say something, looking for a minute like he wanted to take over. Then he thought better of it and sat back down. By this time, Cherry was already wrestling the plane into a ground loop—a tight, barely controlled circle at high speed. The idea was to drain the plane's momentum gradually without hurtling off the airfield into a building. But for the better part of a minute they spun round like a high-speed amusement park ride.

Just below the cockpit, in the navigator's bay, John DeAngelis hung on for dear life. If one of the wheels gave out, the nose of the plane would collapse in a heap on the runway. DeAngelis would be the first thing to hit the ground.

Thanks to Captain Cherry's skills, the navigator

was spared. The high-speed ride came to a smooth stop, and Rickenbacker complimented Cherry on the maneuver.

A tow truck hauled the bomber back to the hangar, and the men began unloading their equipment into another B-17.

The crew were surprised to find they were taking off again as soon as they could transfer the gear. Normally, they'd take a new plane up for a trial run. As engineer, Bartek would spend a couple of hours inspecting it to make sure everything was flight worthy. DeAngelis would get to check his navigation instruments.

Captain Cherry objected to the quick turnaround time, which Bartek was happy to see. That was just like their pilot, always looking out for his crew. But the general in charge said that if the captain was afraid to take on the mission, they would just get another pilot. Cherry was too proud to back down from a challenge, so they all got ready to fly. Whatever this mission was, Bartek figured, it must be important to somebody.

As the cots and mailbags and provisions exited the original plane, Whittaker noticed DeAngelis inspecting a piece of equipment. It was an octant—an instrument used to measure latitude and longitude from thousands of feet in the air. The octant had taken a beating during the ground loop, DeAngelis said.

"Anything wrong with it?" Whittaker asked.

"Doesn't seem to be," the navigator replied.

DeAngelis cradled the octant in his hand and carried it aboard their new plane. By 1:30 a.m., when the nose of the B-17 rose successfully into the sky, he had settled the instrument in place on his new table. There, as the sun rose over the Pacific, he would use it to chart a course for their first refueling stop, Canton Island.

CHAPTER 2

ISLAND EYES

As the plane rumbled into the night, Rickenbacker and Adamson went aft. Two cots had been set up for them in the back—the B-17 version of VIP treatment. They lay down and tried to sleep.

Rickenbacker tossed and turned while he listened to Adamson snore. It had been twenty months since the crash of the passenger plane that had nearly killed him. But his body still ached from the beating it had taken. It was hard to get comfortable in a plush bed, much less an army cot in a rattling bomber. At 10,000 feet, the air outside was below freezing, even in the tropics. He wore a leather flight jacket over his business suit and huddled under an expensive designer coat. Still, he couldn't stop shivering.

It was a demanding, two-day trip across the Pacific, and Rickenbacker wasn't thrilled with the crew he'd been stuck with. Whittaker was broad-shouldered and rugged.

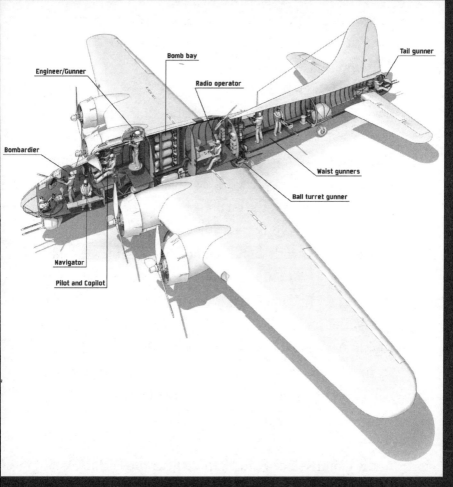

Bomb bay

Tail gunner

Engineer/Gunner

Radio operator

Bombardier

Waist gunners

Ball turret gunner

Navigator

Pilot and Copilot

Rickenbacker's B-17 had been stripped of its guns and ammunition. But when it was fully equipped, the "Flying Fortress" went into battle with 2 tons of bombs and a crew of ten.

But this was a young man's war. Why, Rickenbacker wondered, had they given him a copilot in his forties? And the pilot, Cherry, seemed like a hick, with his cowboy boots and his goatee. His attitude was way too casual for Rickenbacker. A war demanded discipline, not one-liners delivered in a Texas drawl.

As for the rest of them, they were green. DeAngelis, a wiry guy with a pencil mustache, didn't have much experience navigating long flights. Bartek, who had barely opened his mouth so far, only had four months of training as an engineer and precious few flights on a four-engine plane. Kaczmarczyk, the second engineer, had been added to the crew to help Bartek. But he had just spent weeks in the hospital with jaundice and appendicitis. He had a pale, sickly look to him. Reynolds, the radio operator, was the one crew member who seemed to know what he was doing. But a radio operator didn't have much to do on flights near Japanese lines. The enemy had radiomen scanning the airwaves, hoping to pick up news of a vulnerable plane or ship. Silence was the best policy.

———◆———

In the months since Pearl Harbor, the entire Pacific Ocean had become a war zone. After the surprise attack, Japanese ships and aircraft carriers swept south from the home island and bases in Southeast Asia. Guam fell under Axis control, then Wake Island and Hong Kong. The Dutch East Indies were next, and then the Philippines. American troops manning the last line of defense on the Philippine peninsula of Bataan chalked "V"s on their helmets—not for "victory" but for "victim." One British general summed up the result of the onslaught: "It means that from Africa eastwards to America, through the Indian Ocean and the Pacific, we have lost control of the sea."

By the time Rickenbacker was assigned to visit the war zone, the U.S. and their British allies had stopped the offensive. But half the Pacific Ocean belonged to Japan. That meant they were able to maintain a steady supply of rubber and oil and tin to keep the Japanese war machine humming. It also meant that Japan was dangerously close to shutting off the supply route between the U.S. and Australia. If that happened, the entire Eastern Hemisphere could fall under Japanese control.

In October 1942, the two sides, Allies versus Axis, sat balanced on a deadly seesaw. At the center stood an airstrip hacked out of the jungle on an island called Guadalcanal. Ten weeks earlier, 11,000 U.S. Marines had stormed the airfield in the early morning and seized it for the Allies. It was just a single dirt runway—choked with dust in dry weather, mired in mud when it rained. But if the Japanese

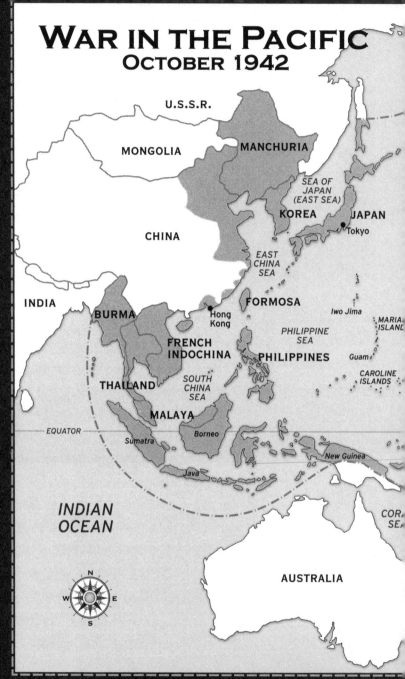

WAR IN THE PACIFIC
OCTOBER 1942

U.S.S.R.

MONGOLIA

MANCHURIA

SEA OF JAPAN (EAST SEA)

KOREA

JAPAN

Tokyo

CHINA

EAST CHINA SEA

INDIA

BURMA

Hong Kong

FORMOSA

Iwo Jima

MARIANA ISLANDS

FRENCH INDOCHINA

PHILIPPINE SEA

PHILIPPINES

Guam

THAILAND

SOUTH CHINA SEA

CAROLINE ISLANDS

MALAYA

EQUATOR

Sumatra

Borneo

New Guinea

Java

INDIAN OCEAN

CORAL SEA

AUSTRALIA

N W E S

After the attack on Pearl Harbor in December 1941, the Japanese navy launched a major offensive in the Pacific. When Rickenbacker and the B-17 crew took off on their mission, Allied forces were trying desperately to push the Japanese back and protect the supply route from the U.S. to Australia.

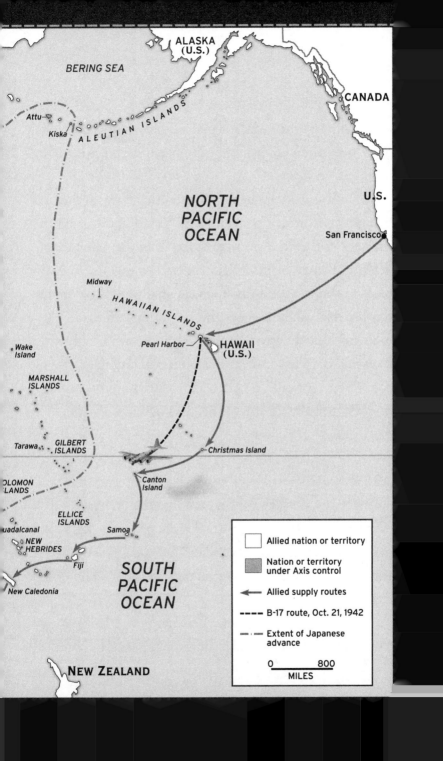

took it back, that would put Samoa and Fiji and New Caledonia in range of their planes. The southern supply route from the U.S. would be chopped in two. Australia would be on its own.

That was exactly the fate Rickenbacker was trying to help prevent. In his pocket, as he tossed and turned in the back of the bomber, were orders from the secretary of defense, Henry Stimson. Rickenbacker was to visit air bases in the war zone, and Guadalcanal was at the top of the list. He would inspect the operations and give pep talks to the exhausted airmen, who were wracked with fever and diarrhea and surviving on two rations of rice a day. Then he would report back to Washington on the best way to gain control of the skies over the Pacific.

———◆———

At 6 a.m., Rickenbacker finally gave up on sleep. He got up, made his way forward, and ran into Kaczmarczyk. Like everyone else, Rickenbacker had given up on the kid's last name and just called him "Alex." Sergeant Alex looked exhausted, so Rickenbacker offered up his cot and continued on.

In the nose of the plane, DeAngelis had been using his octant to take positional readings on the stars. Everything looked good, he said. They were on course to hit Canton Island at 9:30 a.m.

In the cockpit, the mood was upbeat. Rickenbacker took a turn at the controls. He and Captain Cherry compared the B-17 to the rickety planes of World War I. When Rickenbacker fought, he had gone aloft in wood-frame fighters with cotton fabric for a shell. If a pilot dove too fast, the wing fabric shredded in midair. With nothing but a wood skeleton for wings, those planes would plunge for a head-on meeting with the ground. The B-17, with its aluminum shell, felt pretty solid by contrast.

Colonel Adamson came up from the tail, and the four men tried to keep themselves alert with coffee and sweet rolls. At about 8:30, Cherry pointed the plane downward. At 1,000 feet, he leveled off to start looking for Canton Island.

They were still looking an hour later, when DeAngelis popped up from the nose compartment. Under normal circumstances, he had the wiry, nervous energy of a dog on a hunt. Now he was even more agitated. He beckoned Cherry into the navigator's area, and when the two emerged, they both looked worried. DeAngelis had been taking readings on the sun with his octant, and something wasn't right. He felt it had probably been damaged during the failed takeoff the night before. If the octant was off by just 1 degree, they could have missed the island by 20 miles.

Rickenbacker started to feel uneasy. They had been told they had a 10-mile-per-hour tailwind. But down below, angry whitecaps crowned the waves, and 10-mile-per-hour winds don't make seas like that. Suppose the winds were double or triple what they'd been told. They could be 180 miles beyond Canton Island by now.

Cherry sat back down and tried another way to locate their position. He found a radio signal from Canton. Then he asked Whittaker to turn the direction finder antenna fastened to the roof outside the cockpit. The direction finder rotates to pinpoint the position of a station by determining when the signal is weakest and strongest. If they could find where Canton's signal was coming from, they could set a course for it.

Whittaker tugged at the crank inside the cockpit, but it was broken. The antenna wouldn't budge.

Cherry was the first one to say it out loud, and he did it in the way his crew had come to expect. Not a word wasted. No one left guessing what he really meant.

"We're lost," he said.

Bartek checked the readings on the fuel tanks and announced they had about four hours left. Reynolds raised Canton's station on the radio and asked them to use the plane's signal to calculate its position. But Canton didn't have the equipment to trace a radio signal. Reynolds tried a few more wireless stations. But the only island he was able to contact was at least 1,000 miles to the northeast. Their fuel reserve would only get them three-quarters of the way there, and they'd be left no closer to civilization than they were right now.

With less than four hours of flying time left, Cherry started "boxing the compass." He climbed to 5,000 feet and put the bomber on a course to fly forty-five minutes in each direction of the compass. It was standard procedure for a lost plane, and it allowed the crew to scan as wide an area as possible in a limited amount of time. Cherry took care to turn south first. Five hundred miles to the west and north of Canton lay the Gilbert Islands, where the Japanese had established a base. North of that was nothing but enemy waters.

Whittaker, Bartek, Adamson, and Alex scanned the sea for signs of land. DeAngelis relayed messages back and forth between Reynolds in the radio room and Cherry in his pilot's seat. Before long, Rickenbacker suggested a trick he recalled from World War I. Reynolds instructed Canton to fire their antiaircraft guns with the shells set to detonate at 8,000 feet. Cherry nosed the B-17 up to 10,000 feet, where they looked for the telltale bursts of smoke. If they could spot smoke, they would find the island below it.

There was nothing but blue sky and clouds as far as they could see.

As he gazed out the tiny portal, looking for any sign of civilization, Whittaker thought this must be the loneliest, emptiest place in the world. The Pacific Ocean covers a third of the globe's surface. Take all the land in the world, plunk it down in the Pacific, and you would still have room for another piece the size of North America. Canton Island was just a thin ribbon of coral with a lagoon in the middle. It was eight miles long by four miles wide. They were looking for a 32-square-mile patch in 68,000,000 square miles of ocean. Imagine trying to find a quarter in the middle of a football field from the top of the stands.

As they finished the final leg of the box, there was little hope left of finding land. It was time for plan B: ditching the plane in the ocean. Inessentials went out the hatch in the bomb bay. The bulkheads were padded for impact. Emergency supplies were collected by the rear hatch. Cherry and Whittaker planned the landing.

DeAngelis prayed. They all put on standard-issue inflatable life vests. Alex grabbed a special thermos to make sure he had cream for his coffee.

They assigned themselves places in the three rafts. Rickenbacker, Adamson, and Bartek would share one of the large rafts; Cherry, Whittaker, and Reynolds would take the other. DeAngelis and Sergeant Alex, the smallest guys aboard, would take the tiny two-man raft they had stashed in the rear.

As they took their places, Bartek noticed that Adamson was braced against the bulkhead in an awkward position, and he was tempted to say something. But Bartek had never even spoken to anyone ranked higher than a major. He wasn't about to give advice to a colonel.

At some point, as Cherry nosed the plane toward the sea, Rickenbacker and Adamson huddled in the back, already thinking past the landing. If they had missed Canton to the north, they could easily be within range of Japanese planes based in the Gilberts. Army intelligence had told Adamson about a truth serum the Germans had supposedly given to the Japanese. One shot in the arm and a prisoner spilled everything he knew. At least, that was the story.

Rickenbacker knew more than a few Allied secrets—not just about Pacific bases, but about plans for one of the biggest surprise attacks of the war. The Americans and their British allies were secretly preparing an invasion of North Africa, where the Germans and British had been battling in the desert for more than two years. Rickenbacker knew exactly when and where the invasion was going to happen. If that information fell into Japanese hands, the results could be disastrous. He knew he couldn't risk becoming a prisoner of war.

As the plane drew nearer to the water's surface, Adamson and Rickenbacker made a pact. If a Japanese plane found them, drifting in their rafts, they would throw themselves overboard and dive until they drowned. But even that grim plan was based on an optimistic guess: that they would first survive the impact with the unforgiving ocean.

CHAPTER 3

IMPACT

The shock from the crash landing did not last long. In the copilot's seat, seconds after the plane hit the water, Jim Whittaker tore off his safety belt. He turned to see how the rest of the crew had fared. Johnny Bartek had released one of the forward life rafts and was struggling with the other. Whittaker grabbed the pull cord and yanked. The package dislodged from its compartment. A carbon dioxide canister was supposed to uncork automatically and inflate the raft with a whoosh. Whittaker could only hope that when he got outside the raft would be floating on the waves, held fast to the plane by a length of cord.

Whittaker and Cherry moved aft to check on the others. Miraculously, everyone behind them was alive. How long they would stay that way was unclear. The tail of the plane had cracked on impact and listed noticeably toward the ocean floor. Water was shin deep and rising in the main compartment. If they didn't move fast, the plane that had held them aloft for fifteen hours would bury them alive two miles beneath the surface of the sea. They had five minutes—maybe less—to escape the wreckage, get into the rafts, and cut themselves free.

The next moments passed in a blur, each move less a choice than an instinct. Adamson had wrenched his back, as Bartek had feared he would. He was moaning in pain while he struggled to his feet. Reynolds had stayed at the radio till the last second, tapping out the SOS. Blood poured from a gash in his nose as he waded aft toward the hatch. Rickenbacker prodded Adamson through the topside hatch into the light and then followed him out. Alex and DeAngelis shoved the small life raft out and climbed after it. Whittaker and Bartek went out the cockpit hatch. Cherry, the plane's captain till its final moments, emerged last.

Bartek found himself on the right wing, wrestling with one of the forward rafts. Rickenbacker and Adamson made their way toward him along the top of the plane. The sun threw a blinding light off the ocean. Waves twice the height of a man beat against the side of the plane. The ocean had turned the 25-ton bomber into a toy bobbing and weaving at the whim of the water. Bartek

A crashed B-17 after ditching in the waters off New Guinea in 1942.

fought to keep his balance. Somehow it had fallen to him, a mere private, to get the two colonels safely in the raft.

He strained at the rope that kept the raft tethered to the plane, trying to pull it close to the wing. It was no easy job, playing tug-of-war with one hundred pounds of rubberized canvas against an entire ocean. Adamson and Rickenbacker climbed down to the wing. Bartek muscled the raft close, and the injured colonel slid in. He collapsed on the floor of the raft, paralyzed with pain.

Adamson's weight jerked the raft away from the wing and pulled Bartek off his feet. Bartek landed hard and clung to the wing, his legs dangling in the water. Scrambling back to safety, he wrapped the rope around one hand, found a hold on the plane with the other, and held the raft close. Rickenbacker climbed in, and finally, Bartek fell in on top of him.

A moment of relief followed in the tiny raft as they shifted to find a stable arrangement of legs and arms. As soon as Bartek got himself upright he found the rope that still held them fast to the plane. That quarter-inch tether had been their lifeline a moment ago. Now, if they didn't find a way to sever it before the plane went under, the line would drag their only means of survival to the bottom of the sea. Bartek grabbed the line and tried to tear it with his bare hands. This was exactly the kind of life-or-death situation that was supposed to give a person superhuman strength, he thought. Wasn't it?

Thankfully, someone produced a penknife. Bartek cut the line, and they floated free of the sinking plane. Somewhere along the way, grappling with the sharp edges of the B-17, he had sliced the palm of his hand nearly to the bone. The raft had taken on several inches of water. But for the moment they had what they needed—something between them and the bottom of the ocean.

They pieced together the aluminum oars stashed under the inflatable sidewalls of the raft. Rickenbacker took off his hat and bailed salt water mixed with Bartek's blood into the sea.

— ◆ —

As Bartek, Rickenbacker, and Adamson paddled beyond the tail of the plane, they noticed a frenzy of activity on the other side. Captain Cherry, Whittaker, and Reynolds were settled in the other large raft. But DeAngelis and Sergeant Alex had been dumped in the sea by their much smaller craft. Their oars were floating away on the swells.

DeAngelis clung to the raft. He wrestled it upright and pulled himself over the side. Alex thrashed and spluttered, trying to keep his head above water. But with DeAngelis's help he managed to get aboard. After a minute of furious rowing, Cherry and Whittaker corralled the missing oars and returned them to the small raft. Alex promptly leaned over the side and vomited into the ocean.

— ◆ —

Fifty yards downwind of the plane, the men gathered as close as they could with the constant surge of the swells underneath. The air filled with voices, amped by adrenaline.

"Who's got the water?"

No one had taken the water.

"How about the food?"

No one had the food.

All their careful preparation had been wiped from memory by the force of the impact. In their haste to get out, no one had grabbed the supplies they had stacked by the hatch.

The plane, by now, lay heavy in the water. It rose one moment at the crest of a swell, then vanished into a trough, then rose and vanished and rose again. Most likely, the food and the thermoses were floating in several feet of water. Someone suggested a trip back into the plane to find them, but they all agreed it would be too risky.

Rickenbacker unspooled a length of rope he had wrapped around his waist before they ditched. The men rowed close and started tying the rafts in a line. The ocean was a vast and lonely place. Better to face it together than apart.

Whittaker kept one eye on the giant metal Fortress as she struggled against the waves. The wings had disappeared under the water. The nose lingered above the surface as if it were straining for a few final gasps of air.

Jim Whittaker had been a pilot for fifteen years. He was trained to trust his life to the planes he flew. At 10,000 feet above the earth, a bond developed between man and machine. In the air, the B-17 was sturdy and capable. It was sad to see her thrust into an element she wasn't made for.

He turned his attention to the rope for a moment. When he looked up, the plane was gone. He kept his gaze trained on the spot until a few swells had passed. All he could see, from the raft to the horizon, was ocean.

Six minutes had passed since they plunged from the sky.

CHAPTER 4

STRANDED

The ocean carried the rafts as if they were cars on a roller coaster: 12 feet up to the crest of a swell, 12 feet down to the base of a trough. The men strained at the ropes that bound the rafts together and huddled in tight formation.

They bobbed on the waves, packed like sardines marinating in salt water. Blood had begun to dry in a brown crust across Reynolds's face. Bartek was still bleeding from his hand. Adamson could barely move in the corner of his raft.

And yet, they were alive. For the moment, nothing else mattered. As the plane headed for its meeting with the ocean, each member of the crew had lived with the probability that he would be dead in a few minutes. But here they were, still breathing the air. And that was enough to fill each of them with pure joy. The simple fact of survival made the world look hopeful.

And then the retching began.

As the churning of the current took its toll, seasickness set in. One by one the men joined Alex at the sides of the rafts, vomiting into the water. Rickenbacker claimed he felt fine. But Whittaker was sure he saw three heads, not just two, bent over the side of the colonel's raft.

Whittaker was enjoying a moment of relief when a sudden movement in the water caught his eye. Since they landed he'd been focused on either the plane in the distance or the raft beneath him. Now he scanned the water around them, and what he saw made him recoil in terror. The ocean was not as lonely as he had thought.

Everywhere he looked, triangular fins sliced the surface. Sharks, long, sleek, and silent, surrounded the rafts. When a wave crested just right, Whittaker got a good look at them. They were gray on top, white on the bottom. Some were at least ten or twelve feet long—even longer than the rafts. They circled the group like vultures waiting for an easy victim.

It was suddenly clear to Whittaker just how vulnerable he and the rest of the crew were. If the sharks decided to attack, the rafts would give way in a second. The rubberized canvas was tough, but it was no match for a set of shark teeth. One good bite and the men would have more holes to patch than they could manage.

The Predators: Whittaker thought some of the sharks circling the rafts resembled tiger sharks.

Even fully inflated, the rafts were barely any protection at all. The side tubes were little more than a foot tall and a foot wide. The two-person raft was so small that DeAngelis and Alex had trouble keeping their elbows from dangling over the side.

The men pulled their limbs in tight and kept a wary eye on the waters around them. The predators seemed willing to keep their distance—for now.

———◉———

As their stomachs settled, the men regrouped to discuss their prospects. Still flush with adrenaline from the narrow escape, everyone felt sure they would be home soon. The occasional seabird swooped and squawked in the sky overhead. They all agreed that gulls didn't stray far from land; there had to be an island nearby. Besides, they had been in contact with Canton till the very end. The radio operator there had assured them that planes had already been sent to look for them. Then there was the SOS signal Reynolds had banged out till the very last moment. Rickenbacker insisted that someone must have heard it and gotten a read on their position.

Young Johnny Bartek, for one, was convinced it wouldn't be more than three days before they were rescued. If they were nothing but no-name enlisted troops, they'd be on their own, he thought. But they had the VIP of all VIPs with them. The generals would send the whole army out to look for Rickenbacker. A stream of planes would be dispatched from California to Hawaii, Hawaii to Canton. From there the rescue parties would fan out over the ocean, spotters peering out the windows. The tops of the rafts were painted bright yellow to make them stand out against the waves. Before long, they would all be sitting under palm trees somewhere, sipping pineapple juice and trading stories about the ordeal. Bartek could get home to his grieving family.

In fact, with any luck, they'd be off the rafts before sundown. That way they wouldn't have to spend a night at sea.

In the meantime, they took stock of their supplies. Before they ditched, DeAngelis had gone through all the parachutes on the plane and stripped them of anything useful. The haul consisted of several fishhooks and some line, a supply of quinine in case they got malaria, and a metal tin full of matches. The fishhooks, at least, might prove useful—if they could find bait. All they had for food, however, were four oranges and a handful of chocolate bars. The chocolate had been in Alex's pocket when he took a dip in the ocean. The salt water had turned it into a vile green mush that no one was willing to touch.

Rounding out their worldly possessions were the following items: eight inflatable life vests; two sheath knives, a pen knife, and a pair of pliers; eighteen flares and a Very pistol to fire them; two .45 caliber pistols and some ammunition; three sets of aluminum oars; two collapsible rubber bailing buckets; two hand pumps and three patch kits to keep the rafts inflated; a few pencils; and, finally, a pocket compass and a map of the Pacific.

For the next few hours, a steady banter made its way across the waves. The men debated where in the world they might be—how close to the nearest land, how far from Japanese lines.

Their seating arrangements were good for a few laughs. The "large" rafts were supposedly made to fit five people. Five Pygmies maybe, Whittaker thought, but average-sized humans? Whoever made the puny things had scammed the army out of a good sum of money. The two large rafts measured four feet by seven feet on the outside. Inside the inflatable sidewalls, there was barely enough room for one man to lie lengthwise. Three men could wedge themselves in with an architecture so elaborate it was hard to tell which limbs belonged to whom.

The smaller raft produced even more amusement. They called it the "doughnut," and that's about how big it seemed. Alex and DeAngelis made themselves at home by sitting face-to-face and threading their legs over and under each other's arms.

The Rafts: A demonstration of the cramped seating arrangements in the "large" raft (top) and the "doughnut" (bottom).

As the sun sank toward the horizon, the men shifted and squirmed and got ready for a night at sea. Rickenbacker suggested they keep watch in two-hour shifts. To keep spirits up, he offered $100 to the first man who spotted a ship, a plane, or an island.

The sun disappeared in the west, and a three-quarter moon rose in its place. The sharks vanished in the half-light. But they were still out there, silent, vigilant. One by one the men fell silent, too. To Rickenbacker, there was something about the vast darkness that made all conversation lose its meaning.

At some point, Cherry loaded a flare in the Very pistol, aimed at the heavens, and fired. For a moment, a bright, crimson light outshone the moon and the stars. Then it was gone, and no light from a rescue plane appeared to replace it. The night seemed even darker than it had before.

CHAPTER 5

THINGS THAT GO BUMP IN THE NIGHT

The water turned an inky black that night, and Eddie Rickenbacker couldn't sleep. An entire world throbbed beneath the three tiny rafts. At its average, the Pacific Ocean runs two and a half miles deep. In 1942, the Empire State Building stood as the tallest human-made structure in the world. Clouds sometimes obscured the tip of its spire. And yet, almost nine Empire State Buildings, stacked one atop the other, would fit between the rafts and the bottom of the ocean. There were creatures the size of buses down there. If a curious humpback whale decided to surface in the wrong place, the men would be scattered helpless on the waves.

Then, of course, there were the sharks.

Rickenbacker felt the first impact shortly after dark. Something swept past from below and bumped the flexible canvas floor of the raft. Then it happened again. A tail or a head broke the surface of the water a few feet away. Then another bump from below.

One after another, the sharks that had been following them took turns scraping against the bottom of the rafts. When one hit just right, the men could feel the impact on the backs of their legs—just a fraction of an inch of rubberized canvas between human flesh and predator. Sometimes the sharks rocked the rafts with a flip of their tails before vanishing again in the dark.

Tiger sharks can grow up to 16 feet long and can weigh more than 1,500 pounds. Their jaws are powerful enough to crack a sea turtle's shell.

It wasn't clear whether they were looking for a meal, but no one wanted to find out. The rafts felt insubstantial next to 1,000 pounds of muscle and teeth. Rickenbacker worried that the rough, scaly hide of a particularly aggressive shark could shred the canvas, leaving nothing between him and a swarm of ravenous killers. And so he lay in the moonlight, wide awake, waiting for the next nudge from below.

Sleep would have been a welcome relief from the conditions in the raft. Rickenbacker's bed was barely the size of a bathtub—and he was sharing it with two grown men. Colonel Adamson, whose back was in bad shape, lay curled in one end. Rickenbacker and Bartek tossed and turned in the other half, trying to find an alignment they could live with. Every move they made provoked a groan from Adamson. One badly placed elbow, and the groans turned into a foul-mouthed grumbling.

But even if Adamson hadn't been there—if the raft had been as big as a bedroom and equipped with a mattress, if the sharks had merely been tropical fish splashing about in the waves—Rickenbacker still would not have slept. They had agreed on a schedule of watch duty. But what if Bartek or Reynolds or DeAngelis dozed off and slept through the hum of a passing plane? What if Sergeant

Eddie as a kid in Columbus, Ohio. He grew up poor, often scrounging coal from the train yard to help heat the house.

Alex mistook the lights of a ship for a pair of stars on the horizon?

It didn't come naturally to Eddie Rickenbacker to leave his fate in someone else's hands. His parents had been dirt-poor when they arrived in Columbus, Ohio, from Switzerland. His mother cleaned other people's laundry to pay back a $300 loan for their first house. By the time he was five, Eddie was hawking newspapers to help support the family.

To heat the house, he and his brother scrounged for coal dropped from passing trains. He grew up believing that you survived in this world on your own strength, knowledge, and initiative. A race car driver had his pit crew. A pilot had expert mechanics. But when it came down to it, there was just the driver, the car, and the road; the pilot, the plane, and the sky.

Eddie Rickenbacker was convinced of one thing above all others: There was only one person he could rely on, and that was Eddie Rickenbacker.

Finally, dawn came and the world began to lighten. A gray mist hung over the rafts as the air began to warm. They had been shivering all night in the cold salt spray, but now their bodies slowly began to heat up.

The sharks, however, were still with them, circling like vultures. Shouting across the swells, the men tried to figure out whether their stalkers saw them as prey or just a curiosity. The U.S. Army taught its fliers that sharks aren't a danger to humans. But maybe the generals were just trying to calm their nerves. After all, the newspapers had a habit of referring to the Pacific as "shark-infested waters." In early August, Japanese ships had sunk three American cruisers and a destroyer off Guadalcanal. Rumor had it that many of the 1,500 men lost had been eaten by sharks.

Bartek, for one, was convinced the predators were looking for a chance to turn the men into dinner. Rickenbacker wasn't so sure. He spotted a six-inch leech of some kind on one of the shark's heads. He and Whittaker thought that when the sharks bumped the rafts from below they were simply trying to scrape the parasites off their backs.

As yet, no one was willing to jump in and test the theories. When an arm or a leg strayed close to the side of a raft, it was hastily yanked back in.

———◆———

As the day brightened, Rickenbacker had the men pull the rafts close. No one mentioned it, but the old war hero had taken charge since they ditched the plane. His arrogance rubbed some of the men the wrong way. They were fiercely loyal to Cherry, and by the rules of the military the captain of the plane was in charge until the mission was over. But there was something about Rickenbacker that commanded attention. When he spoke there was no doubt in his voice. To seven men stranded in the middle of the ocean, certainty was a comforting thing.

With the rafts clustered tight, Rickenbacker launched into a pep talk. He was convinced they would be rescued soon.

"The planes are probably taking off right now, and that $100 is still up," he said.

In the meantime, he warned, they had to conserve energy: move around as little as possible; don't speak too much; try to protect themselves from the sun. Most of all, don't drink the seawater, no matter how thirsty they got. Seawater is a lot saltier than the fluids in the human body. Drink it, and the body actually loses liquid trying to flush out the excess salt. The men would dehydrate faster drinking salt water than drinking nothing at all.

They had to be disciplined about everything, Rickenbacker said, including food. It had been twenty-four hours since Rickenbacker, Adamson, Cherry, and Whittaker sat in the cockpit feasting on sweet rolls and coffee. The other men hadn't eaten since before they took off from Hawaii.

Captain Cherry dragged out their supplies, and they did the math, simple and grim: Four oranges, eight people; half an orange per person.

Rickenbacker proposed that they eat one orange every other day, dividing each one evenly eight ways. Reynolds and DeAngelis grumbled that they hadn't had breakfast the day before like the men in the cockpit.

"If we'd known that before we went down, we'd have taken care of you," Rickenbacker replied. "But now it's too late."

The protest died away. They'd be rescued before they got to the second orange anyway. Wouldn't they?

Cherry handed the supplies to Rickenbacker. Seven men watched while the colonel pulled out a sheath knife, bent over an orange, and carved it like a jeweler into eight precisely equal pieces.

Most of the men ate their entire ration, peel and all. Rickenbacker and Cherry thought of another use for the peel. They pulled out the hooks and line that DeAngelis had salvaged from the parachute sacks. Each man baited a hook with a small piece of peel and threw it overboard.

They watched while the lines trailed the raft, dangling the bright orange bait in the waves. The peel did not attract a single fish.

Whittaker's watch, which miraculously still worked, ticked away the hours. The sun burned off the mist, and by 11 a.m. its glow ruled the sky. Four hours ago, they had welcomed the warmth. Now the heat was unbearable.

Whittaker stripped off his undershirt and soaked it in the ocean. He draped it over his head and felt the cool water run down his face. Moments later he was sweating under the makeshift canopy, losing precious liquid with each bead that appeared on his face. He tried holding the shirt inches above his head to let the breeze blow through.

As the heat bore down, the wind picked up. The rafts rode the waves at an uneven pace. One minute Whittaker's raft pulled ahead, jerking the rafts on the other end of the line. A minute later, it lagged, banging into Rickenbacker, Adamson, and Bartek. That brought the doughnut rocketing in from behind, with DeAngelis and Alex clinging to its flimsy sidewalls.

Every bump nudged tempers closer to the edge. Knees were forced into backs and elbows into heads. Skin already raw with salt water chafed against canvas. Adamson growled in pain. Bartek complained that he didn't have enough space. Someone else moaned about the heat. Before long angry sniping filled the air between the rafts.

Captain Cherry made a makeshift sail with his T-shirt and two oars. It seemed to help keep the rafts apart. But it didn't solve the real problem. The men were getting anxious, and it wasn't just the close quarters or the heat. More than anything, it was the empty sky above them.

As sunset approached they had been drifting for more than twenty-four hours without a plane or boat in sight. The scorching heat receded, and in its place came the nagging feeling that they had been cavalier about their chances of being rescued. The base at Canton had no idea where they were. What if no one else had picked up their SOS?

The men couldn't help replaying the sequence of events that had dropped them into the sea. Captain Cherry, DeAngelis, and Bartek felt it all could have been avoided if they had taken their time after the first plane failed. The octant could have been replaced, the new plane inspected, and the direction finder fixed. There was no point in saying it, but the thought was in the air like the whine of a mosquito: If Rickenbacker hadn't been in such a hurry, they would be safely en route from Canton to the western Pacific right now.

But that wasn't Rickenbacker's way. If you travel when there's a war on, he believed, you have to be willing to take risks. The enemy doesn't wait for engineers to check everything and check it again. There was no time for "prissy safeguards" in the army.

And so here they were, stranded somewhere in the central Pacific. DeAngelis had taken readings on the stars the night before. Now, with Whittaker's watch, he checked the exact time of the sunset. Five minutes earlier than the night before, he claimed, meant they had drifted 50 miles during the day. In fact, they had traveled about 25 or 30, probably west and a little south.

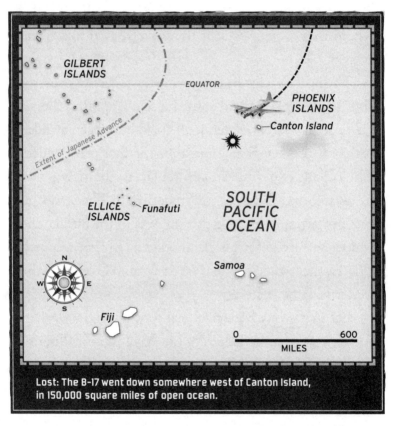

GILBERT ISLANDS

EQUATOR

PHOENIX ISLANDS

Canton Island

Extent of Japanese Advance

ELLICE ISLANDS

Funafuti

SOUTH PACIFIC OCEAN

N
W   E
S

Samoa

Fiji

0   600
MILES

Lost: The B-17 went down somewhere west of Canton Island, in 150,000 square miles of open ocean.

But where had they started? Rickenbacker pulled out the map of the Pacific, which had so far stayed dry enough to read. He and Cherry thought they had gone down west and north of Canton, which put them dangerously close to enemy waters. The Japanese-held Gilbert Islands lay five or six hundred miles west and a little north of Canton. If they were right, they could easily be within range of Japanese planes.

DeAngelis believed they were south of Canton. If he was right, they might be beyond the enemy's reach. But it also meant they were floating in a large triangle of empty ocean. Canton—the only inhabited land in the Phoenix Islands—lay at the northeast point of the triangle. The Gilberts occupied the northwest point. Another 600 miles to the south lay the Ellice Islands.

They were lost in a vast no-man's-land. In the entire triangle, not a single tiny crest of land broke the surface of the ocean. No regular shipping lanes crossed anywhere near their position. The supply route to Australia ran through Fiji and Samoa, another 500 miles south of the Ellices.

One by one the men confronted a grim possibility: They could be completely on their own. There might be planes up there searching for them. But inside that triangle lay 150,000 square miles of empty ocean. They hadn't been able to find an entire island when they were circling up there. Would the search planes really be able to spot three tiny rafts?

They began to calculate their chances of finding land. If they were headed southwest, they might run into the Ellice Islands. But that entire island chain made up only 10 square miles of land. It would take a miracle to wash up on 10 square miles of sand and coral in 68 million square miles of water.

Rickenbacker spoke up with his own calculations. He claimed they could make it to Fiji, a much larger target, in eighteen to twenty-five days. He didn't really believe it himself, and eighteen days with no food, water, or shelter seemed like an eternity. But Rickenbacker felt that the men needed something to hope for. Fiji would have to do.

As darkness fell, conversation trailed off. Bartek had stashed a Bible with a zippered cover in his pocket before they left the plane. Now he dug it out and read to himself. Captain Cherry pulled out the Very pistol to send up a different kind of prayer. He stuck a flare in the barrel and aimed at the sky. The first one went nowhere. The second rose and burned for a few seconds before dropping into the sea. The third rose high, floated on its parachute, and turned the sky bright red for a minute and a half. For several minutes after it burned out they peered into the darkness, hoping that a star might turn into the taillight of a plane.

Finally, they settled in for another sleepless night. Adamson took out a pencil and scratched the date on the sidewall of the raft: *Thursday, October 22.*

The nearest piece of the mainland United States lay at least 4,000 miles away, and the men could only wonder what their families were doing. It would have been midnight in California. Whittaker's daughter, Shirley, would be in bed. What would his son, Thomas, be up to at the navy base in San Francisco? In Texas it was 2 a.m., and Cherry's five-year-old daughter, Paula, was surely asleep. What about Rickenbacker's wife, Adelaide, in New York? And Bartek's parents in their New Jersey house, where his sister's bed now lay empty? Did they know yet what had happened to the B-17? The men hoped it hadn't made the newspapers, because the headlines would surely declare them dead. But had their families gotten a phone call from the army? A telegram? Or the most ominous messenger of all: a man in uniform knocking at the front door?

CHAPTER 6

DEAD CALM

For Adelaide Rickenbacker, the news came on Friday, October 23, in a phone call. It was General "Hap" Arnold, head of the Army Air Forces. He was calling to say her husband was lost.

"*. . . 14 hours SSW of Oahu. May have overshot island. Hour's fuel.*"

That was the last the world had heard from Eddie.

Adelaide spent that day and the next sitting by the phone in her New York City apartment, feeling useless. She called her sons, David and William, at boarding school to give them the news. Friends called and visited, and sometimes she let herself cry. For newspaper reporters she tried to sound upbeat. "Eddie will turn up," she said. "He's too old a hand to get lost in any airplane now."

On Saturday, the rest of America woke to the headlines. In New York City: "Rickenbacker Missing in Pacific On Flight Southwest of Hawaii." In Stockton, California:

Adelaide eyes a famous portrait showing Eddie in better days, as a WWI hero.

"American Ace of Aces Missing." In Doylestown, Pennsylvania: "Famed Ace Has Again Crossed Path of Fate." There was no mention anywhere of Bartek or Whittaker or the rest of the crew. The army hadn't named them, or even said how many people were aboard the plane.

For the time being, Rickenbacker was the man in the spotlight. He was "Captain Eddie," or just plain "Eddie" in many of the articles, as though he'd been an old friend to everyone. But Eddie was no ordinary friend. He was a "daredevil of the skies," a "living legend," "the idol of millions," a "great and far-seeing man in the best of our pioneer tradition."

No one was ready to give up on him yet. Over morning coffee, people read about the rafts with their bright yellow coloring and their emergency supplies. Supposedly, downed fliers had stayed alive for weeks at sea—though none of those survivors were named. And maybe it didn't matter, the papers speculated, because Eddie was in a class by himself. He had cheated death so many times before. Why should this time be any different?

"May His Luck Continue to Hold!" proclaimed the *Mobile Register* in Alabama. "Those who loved Captain Rickenbacker and enjoyed his zest for living, and fearless courage," the writer went on, "will never be able to believe him dead, no matter how long he may be missing."

Most of the articles, however, reminded everyone that another famous flier had gone down five years earlier in the same part of the Pacific. This pilot had been attempting the last leg of a round-the-world flight when she lost contact with Howland Island, about 400 miles northwest of Canton. *"We must be on you, but cannot see you— but gas is running low"* was one of her final radio transmissions.

Her name was Amelia Earhart, and she was never heard from again.

Back at sea, the third day dawned in a dead calm. The ocean flattened into a gleaming mirror, broken only by the occasional shark fin.

In a way, the change came as a relief. The 12-foot swells had turned the last two days into constant turmoil, salt spray flying and rafts banging into one another. The crazy ride made it impossible for the men to get their bearings on the world. Climb to the crest of a wave, and you commanded the entire ocean. Drop into a trough and you couldn't see the next raft on the end of a twenty-foot tether. Now water stretched on all sides to the horizon, where it blended with the blue of the sky.

Beautiful.

Restful.

But it was getting them no closer to land.

Cherry's T-shirt was a poor excuse for a sail in a stiff breeze. With no wind at all it was useless. Rowing was exhausting and didn't seem to get them anywhere. At this rate, they wouldn't make five miles a day; Fiji was nothing but a prayer.

As the sun climbed and the mist evaporated, the men fought off the heat however they could. Rickenbacker passed around a few handkerchiefs that he had grabbed from his suitcase before the plane went down. The men tied them around their faces like bandits.

No matter what they did, the sun roasted every inch of exposed skin. Whittaker and DeAngelis had dark complexions that kept them from burning too badly. But the rest of the crew began to look like lobsters—especially Reynolds, who had stripped to his shorts and thrown away his clothes. Rickenbacker actually thought he could smell flesh burning.

As the day wore on, conversation dropped off. The men slumped deep in the rafts. From time to time someone baited a hook with an orange peel and let it dangle in the water. Everyone had stopped insisting they were about to be rescued.

With nothing to do, boredom set in. Occasionally someone would ask Whittaker what time it was. He would check his watch and announce the hour: *12:15 . . . 1:35 . . . 3:22.* Rickenbacker would growl, "Well, there it is. Are you going somewhere?"

At some point Adamson remembered that he had stuck a *Reader's Digest* in his hip pocket before they ditched. He couldn't get in position to extract it himself, so Bartek did it for him. Salt water had turned the entire magazine into a lump of sodden paper, but one article was still readable.

The salvaged page told the story of a balloon flight over France by the famous aviator Alberto Santos-Dumont. Dumont, apparently, had packed a fine meal for his flight, and the writer was fascinated by it. There was chicken, lobster, ice cream, and champagne, each described in mouthwatering detail.

Adamson tortured himself for a minute or two. Then he thrust the magazine at Rickenbacker, who tore off a small piece, baited a hook with it, and threw it to the fish.

For the second day in a row, no one caught a thing.

Mostly the men lay around in a stupor. Occasionally someone would drift off, start to slide into the ocean, and jolt awake, grabbing frantically at a raft mate to stay in the boat. Then he would settle in again, tired from the effort.

All day, limbs felt too heavy to move. Minds drifted, lazy and vague. But little by little, one gnawing obsession crowded out all other thoughts. Every one of the men—Rickenbacker and Adamson, Bartek and Reynolds, Whittaker and Cherry, DeAngelis and Sergeant Alex—began to think compulsively about food.

That was only natural. They had begun the long, slow process of starving to death.

CHAPTER 7

TO CATCH A FISH

O n the morning of the fourth day at sea, Rickenbacker divided the second orange and passed the meager sections around. By this time Bartek, DeAngelis, Reynolds, and Alex had gone close to ninety-six hours with nothing but an eighth of an orange to eat. Under normal circumstances they took in 2,500 calories a day. In the last four days, they had consumed 20.

Under their reddening skin, blood and liver, muscles and brain waged a battle against starvation. On a normal diet, the body converts food into glucose, a form of sugar, and consumes it for energy. The men had exhausted the supply of food in their bodies three days ago. Since then, their cells had been burning stored fat for energy instead of glucose. Already their faces had begun to thin. Bones looked a little more prominent. Now their bodies dug deeper for fuel. Their vital organs harvested protein from muscle tissue in order to keep functioning. Without a new supply of fuel, each man's body was literally consuming itself to stay alive.

Rickenbacker's speech to the men took on a different tone this morning. "You might as well sit down and prepare for a long ride," he told them. They would end up on an island somewhere if they drifted long enough; there was no question in his mind about that. The challenge would be to survive until they did.

<hr />

The men were fast discovering the cruel irony behind being stranded in the ocean: They were starving, and yet they were surrounded by food. The water teemed with sleek, silvery fish—from tiny fingerlings to foot-long jack mackerel and plump-looking dolphins. Sea birds circled overhead, diving occasionally to catch their lunch. The men seemed to have attracted their own traveling ecosystem. But all of it lay just beyond their reach.

They had fishhooks and line, but without food they had no bait; and without bait they had no food. The orange peels held no interest at all for the fish. Rickenbacker tried adding Adamson's shiny key chain as a lure. Whittaker tied his ring to a line and sunk it. Sometimes a fish would get curious and hover near a hook—so close the men could almost taste it. Each time, it would lose interest and dart away.

They debated trying to turn the tables on the sharks and convert the fearsome predators into prey. Cherry could probably put a bullet into one of them at close range. But if he didn't kill it, what would happen? The wounded creature would flail around, trailing blood in the water. Imagine the twelve-foot monsters thrashing around the rafts, whipped into a frenzy by the scent of blood.

They decided it was best to let the sharks be.

The sea birds were another source of frustration. At first they had seemed a surefire sign that land was near. Now it was clear the men had misunderstood the habits of sea birds. These creatures were perfectly at home many miles from land. They taunted the men, darting and hovering in sight but well out of reach. It's not as though the scrawny birds would be much of a meal. But if they could just get their hands on one, they might be able to use the meat for bait. Cherry kept his .45-caliber pistol in his lap during the day. Every now and then he'd take a shot, but he never came close to hitting a bird.

Bartek tormented himself by watching the birds fish. They'd flap low, scanning for prey, and then drop with a splash. An instant later they rose with a meal—just like that. Bartek wasn't normally much of a philosopher. But his sister's death, and now his own close encounter with the end, had pushed his mind to a dark place. All around them, creatures with brains no bigger than the tip of Bartek's little finger found food with ease. Here they were, eight members of the smartest species on Earth. Between them they had decades of education and specialized training. Bartek himself knew how to fix some of the most complex machines ever made.

But out here it was all meaningless.

All they could do was pray that a careless bird might drop a fish in their laps.

———◆———

Day four turned to five and five to six. Adamson could barely move his arms, but each day he scratched the date onto the side of the raft: *October 24 . . . October 25 . . . October 26.* The men started passing Bartek's Bible around and choosing passages to read. Whittaker mostly kept his mouth shut when they did. He wasn't a believer. What good was praying going to do? They were on their own out here.

Each night they sent up flares until they got one to work. When it burned out and left them in darkness, it made them feel like the only people left in the world.

On the fifth morning they gave up on Rickenbacker's rationing plan and ate the third orange. It was dry as the inside of their mouths. The last one started to rot, and they devoured it on the sixth day.

Now the real torture set in. For the first few days they had at least been able to look forward to something—even if it was a tasteless piece of orange they could eat in one bite. By the time the sun baked off the chill of the fifth night and began to roast them alive, they had nothing left but a relentless need for food. They were desperately thirsty, too. But right now, it was hunger that held them captive every waking minute of the day.

As if they could lay out their fantasies on a table and carve them up, the men dreamed up five-course meals in their heads and shared them with one another. Captain Cherry posed as a waiter at one of San Francisco's finest restaurants. He went around the rafts "taking orders." There was always fruit juice to start, then steaks and roasts and chops and turkey. Everyone wanted lemon, their bodies starving for vitamin C. The milkshakes from the officer's club at Hickam Field were in high demand, and strawberry was the flavor of choice.

If they ever got off the rafts, they agreed, they'd all have one another over for dinner. Bartek offered up his mother's Polish meatballs and cabbage, with apple pie for

Americans!
SHARE THE MEAT
as a wartime necessity

To meet the needs of our armed forces and fighting allies, a Government order limits the amount of meat delivered to stores and restaurants.

To share the supply fairly, all civilians are asked to limit their consumption of beef, veal, lamb, mutton and pork to 2½ lbs. per person per week.

YOUR FAIR WEEKLY SHARE

Men, women and children over 12 yrs. old . . . . **2½** Pounds per week

Children 6 to 12 yrs. old . . . . **1½** Pounds per week

Children under 6 yrs. old . . . . **¾** Pound per week

You can add these foods to your share: liver, sweetbreads, kidneys, brains and other variety meats; also poultry and fish.

HELP WIN THE WAR!
Keep within your share

FOODS REQUIREMENT COMMITTEE
War Production Board

Claude R. Wickard
Chairman

OWI Poster No. 10   Additional copies may be obtained upon request from the Division of Public Inquiries, Office of War Information, Washington, D.C.

Back at home, civilians were living on war rations that would have seemed like a king's feast to the men on the rafts.

dessert. DeAngelis said his mother would make spaghetti. Reynolds invited everyone to his parents' ranch in northern California, where they'd feast on fried chicken, followed by cake and pie.

Bartek managed to keep his sense of humor for a while. When the men in the Air Transport Command traveled, they collected $6 a day from the army for expenses. One thing about being lost at sea, Bartek said—the expenses were pretty light. He ended every day by tallying up their earnings.

"Well," he'd say, "that's another six dollars for us."

It was good for a few laughs. But nothing could keep their minds off food for long.

———◆———

Rickenbacker watched with irritation as hunger and exhaustion tore away at the morale of the crew. Simple tasks took almost heroic effort—and the rafts required constant attention. Between the sea spray and tiny leaks in the canvas, water collected incessantly at their feet. To stay afloat, everyone had to help bail out the rafts. They used the collapsible rubber buckets and sometimes their hats to shovel water back into the sea, only to watch it fill the bottom of the rafts again.

When they weren't bailing, someone was laboring over the hand pump, trying to keep invisible leaks from deflating the rafts. During the first couple of days, it was a fifteen-minute task to get the side tubes fully blown up. Now, one man had trouble finishing it without handing the pump over to a raft mate and collapsing from fatigue.

It was hard work just staying afloat, and the men were beginning to wonder if there was any point in doing it. Despite Rickenbacker's pep talks, DeAngelis had decided after the third day that they were pretty much doomed. Pain had turned Adamson into a bitter, grumbling lump in the corner of Rickenbacker's raft. Radioman Jim Reynolds, who was thin to begin with, had started to waste away. He barely said a word and looked like he wouldn't last long without food.

Sergeant Alex looked the worst of the lot. A white paste had formed at the corners of his mouth. He sat in the doughnut and moaned for water or mumbled the name of his girlfriend over and over. Her nickname was Snooks, and it took a while for the men to figure out what he was talking about.

Finally, Rickenbacker got tired of listening to the moaning. In his mind, despair was a contagious disease, and Alex was showing symptoms. If they were going to survive out here, everyone had to believe it was not just possible but certain. Any sign of doubt had to be stamped out quickly and ruthlessly. No one could be allowed to quit.

He roped the doughnut in close and lashed out at Alex.

"Why the hell can't you take it?!" he demanded.

After all, Alex wasn't the only one suffering. And there were thousands more boys out there fighting for their lives in unbearable conditions—American soldiers stuck in waterlogged foxholes eating meager rations of rice and beans.

Alex explained meekly that he'd been recovering from jaundice and appendicitis. He'd only been out of the hospital for a couple of weeks, and he'd gotten some kind of lip or gum infection. He also admitted he'd been leaning over the side of the doughnut and drinking the salt water.

"I tried not to, but I had to," he moaned. "I just had to have water."

Rickenbacker turned away and let the doughnut drift back to the end of its twenty-foot tether. They'd better find food and water soon, he thought, or Alex wasn't going to make it.

Hunger filled the empty hours of the day and night. Their minds groped for solutions, real or imagined.

At one point, Cherry was baiting a hook with yet another useless piece of orange peel when he wondered out loud if fingernails would work as bait.

Bartek said no, it would take a real piece of flesh to make a fish bite.

"What part would you use?" asked Whittaker.

Bartek claimed he'd use an earlobe because they don't serve any purpose.

"You'd never miss it," he said.

Whittaker suggested the tip of a finger.

Reynolds wanted to use a piece of toe because no one would ever notice it was missing.

It had started as idle chatter, but everyone knew it was a real option. They needed bait, and if they had to use their own flesh, shouldn't they do it?

Adamson warned that the blood from a fingertip or an earlobe might aggravate the sharks. That didn't seem like much of a threat after a week at sea with their constant companions. But no one was quite ready to slice off an earlobe for the chance of catching a fish. The conversation passed with all body parts intact.

The talk of using human flesh as bait, however, brought them uncomfortably close to a last-ditch measure that no

THE ILLUSTRATED LONDON NEWS

REGISTERED AT THE GENERAL POST-OFFICE FOR TRANSMISSION ABROAD.

No. 2370.—VOL. LXXXV.   SATURDAY, SEPTEMBER 20, 1884.   WITH EXTRA SUPPLEMENT   SIXPENCE. By Post, 6½d.

THE LOSS OF THE YACHT MIGNONETTE.—FROM SKETCHES BY MR. EDWIN STEPHENS, THE MATE.

The way in which they stowed themselves in the dinghy.

Sailing before the wind ; How the dinghy was managed during the last nine days.

How the dinghy was managed in the heavy weather; with the stern sheets up aft, and the "sea anchor," made of the water-breaker bed and the head-sheets grating.

The survivors of the yacht *Mignonette* shocked the world in 1884 when the news came out that they had killed and eaten their cabin boy.

one was willing to mention aloud. At sea, when men grew desperate enough, they had been known to eat one another to survive.

In 1820, the whale ship *Essex* was rammed by a giant sperm whale about 2,500 miles east of where the three rafts were now drifting. In three months lost at sea, the eight survivors of the *Essex* consumed seven of their companions. In one case, they didn't even wait for a boat mate to die. They drew lots, and the unlucky sailor who picked the short stick was sacrificed for a meal. They drew again to decide who would shoot him. The practice was common enough that it was part of an unwritten code known as the Custom of the Sea. As long as the lots were drawn fairly, no court of law considered it murder.

Most sailors had to be on the verge of death before they resorted to cannibalism. But everyone had a different threshold. It took the castaways from the *Essex* two months before they started saving dead bodies for food. In 1884, the crew of the English yacht *Mignonette* lasted twenty days before they killed and ate their seventeen-year-old cabin boy.

Rickenbacker, Whittaker, Bartek, and the rest of the crew had now been adrift for a week.

CHAPTER 8

OUT OF THE SKY

The names of the B-17 crew were released on October 25, five days after the plane vanished. The army and the navy were using every available plane to search for the men. But by now, the papers were declaring them— and their famous passenger—lost for good.

"Only A Wisp Of Hope," reported the *Lewiston Tribune* in Idaho.

"A Star Has Vanished," decreed the *Gadsden Times* in Alabama.

The *Wichita Beacon* in Kansas left no doubt at all: "Rickenbacker Death a Serious Blow," read its headline on October 27, six days after the men disappeared.

Rickenbacker's close friends and relatives weren't ready to write him off just yet. They spoke to reporters or wrote letters to the editor insisting that Eddie would survive this close call, just like he had survived the others.

But most reporters retold the story of Rickenbacker's life as though they were speaking at his funeral. And nearly everyone agreed that the world had lost a great American. According to the papers, Eddie was a role model. He was a hero at a time when Americans needed heroes. He stood for values that seemed especially important to a nation at war.

Eddie was a man of action. "No swivel chair for him, but the pilot's seat and the roar of the motor," wrote one reporter.

"Lead Foot Ed": Rickenbacker at the wheel of a race car, not long before he went overseas in World War I.

Eddie believed in progress. He raced automobiles in the days when just one in fifty Americans owned one. He flew military missions at a time when planes had been around for barely more than a decade. He started a commercial airline when most people were too scared to set foot on a plane.

Eddie wasn't afraid to take risks. In his racing days, a newspaper called him "Lead Foot Ed" because he knew only one way to race: Floor it until you either win or crash. According to an Illinois paper, he was the "bravest of the brave."

Now it appeared he was gone forever. Eddie had been a meteor, blazing his way "across the horizon of human achievement," gushed the reporter from the *Gadsden Times*. "His star arose and dazzled during the First World War and the shining arc of it swept into the war of the present, finally to be smothered in the spume of the restless Pacific."

———◆———

Back on the rafts, Rickenbacker's star was merely dozing when a small seabird—a swallow or a tern—circled the group, came unusually low in the sky, and landed on his hat.

Eddie woke. The bird looked around at the gaunt

creatures in front of him. They stared back. No one spoke. No one moved.

Rickenbacker saw the greed in the eyes of his raft mates and knew exactly what had happened. He raised his right hand as slowly as he could bear. He touched his chin. He raised his hand higher.

When it reached the brim of his hat he made a blind grab for the bird, clamped his fingers around its legs, trapped its body with his other hand, and hung on as though eight lives depended on it.

The bird could not have weighed more than three ounces. But it was food—and more importantly, bait.

Rickenbacker wrung the bird's neck and plucked its feathers. He carved out the intestines and set them aside. Then he carefully cut the rest into eight equal pieces of dark, sinewy meat. The men devoured the tiny bites raw, bones and all. Aside from the four bites of orange they had so carefully rationed, it was the first food to cross their lips in nearly two hundred hours.

The morsels of bird meat were just enough to make their mouths water for more. Rickenbacker handed a slimy piece of seabird intestines into the other large raft. Two baited hooks went overboard, and eight pairs of eyes stared after them. It didn't take long for the dead bird to serve its purpose. Cherry's boat hauled in a fish about 8 to 12 inches long. Rickenbacker caught another about the same size.

The men carved the first fish into portions an inch square and a half-inch thick. They agreed to store the second fish for the next day's meal.

Rickenbacker thought he could feel the mood in the rafts lighten. The tiny chunk of raw fish tasted cool and moist—one of the most delicious things he had ever eaten. Even Alex and Adamson, in all their misery, seemed to revive when the food hit their tongues.

Best of all, the crew had proven they could use their own resourcefulness to survive. They had reached into the vast ocean and plucked food from it. With patience and a little ingenuity they had turned their prison into a pantry. There was an unlimited supply of fish in the sea, and it was theirs for the taking.

———◆———

The food had a noticeably different effect on Whittaker's mood. He enjoyed his two-course meal of tern and fish. But as soon as he finished, another craving took over. His mouth was pasty and dry. His head throbbed. It felt like the sun was baking every last drop of moisture out of him.

The late-afternoon air cooled and brought some relief. But when the sun finally dropped to the horizon, the colors in the sky tormented Whittaker. All he could think of was the expression "He drank in the sunset." The red would be strawberry, the yellow lemon, the purple grape. And he wanted it all with plenty of ice.

The fact was that people had been known to survive two, even three months without food. Rarely did anyone last for two weeks without water.

CHAPTER 9

NOT A DROP TO DRINK

Every night, after Bill Cherry optimistically pointed the Very pistol at the sky and fired, the flare left behind a metal cartridge, about six inches long and an inch in diameter. The men put them to good use. Since they had trouble standing up in the raft, they peed in the cartridges and dumped the contents over the sides.

By the end of the first week, Rickenbacker and Adamson made a decision that comes eventually to people who are dying of dehydration. They would drink their own urine. Had they known a little more about the body's chemistry, they probably would not have made the effort. Urine contains salt and other minerals the body needs to get rid of. Put those minerals back in and the body loses more liquid trying to flush them back out.

But Rickenbacker and Adamson were desperately thirsty. They let their half-full cartridges sit in the sun, hoping that the heat would somehow purify the contents. Then they tried to drink.

They gave up after a couple of sips.

———◆———

By the second week, the intense hunger that gnawed at Rickenbacker, Adamson, and the crew had begun to fade. It's not as though the tiny morsels of food had satisfied them. Their bodies were still wasting away, consuming muscle for fuel. But their cells and organs adapted to the new regimen, learning to make do with less. The men moved slowly to conserve energy. Reactions came seconds later than they should. Thoughts passed through the brain in slow motion. As the body adjusted, the cravings for food came and went. Mostly there was weakness and a dull, familiar ache that became easier and easier to ignore.

In its place rose a desperate, relentless, piercing desire for water.

"The violence of raving thirst has no parallel in the catalogue of human calamities," wrote the first mate of the *Essex,* who survived the wreck of the whale boat in 1820. He described the affliction as a "raging fever of the throat."

Rickenbacker and the others had begun to understand

exactly what he meant. Their saliva turned to a foul-tasting paste in their mouths. Their tongues felt swollen and thick. They wanted to complain bitterly about the lack of water, but if anyone talked for more than a minute his voice shrank to a raw, hoarse whisper.

Water surrounded them. There were trillions of gallons beneath the rafts and a never-ending supply of mist in the air. And yet the salt seemed to leach moisture out of everything it touched. Cherry rubbed oil from behind his ears into the moving parts of his revolver to keep it lubricated. But after a few days the gun was a useless hunk of rusted metal, and he threw it into the sea.

Whittaker felt the lack of water in every pore. His skin seemed to grow tight as it dried. It felt like a fabric stretched snugly over the bones of his face. He had mostly stopped sweating by now; his body didn't have the liquid to spare. But every minute he spent in the sun seemed to drain another precious drop of moisture from his flesh.

Finally, he couldn't take it any longer. They were floating in the biggest swimming pool on Earth. There were still sharks prowling around down there, but they hadn't attacked so far. "What the hell," he said, and slipped over the side into the cool water. He thought he could feel his skin soaking up liquid like a dry sponge.

A minute later, he was still in one piece.

The others joined him, one by one. Even Alex managed to flop over the side and spend a couple of minutes floating in the sea.

In the next few days, DeAngelis would turn into the most dedicated swimmer of them all. When he went over the side, he would drop a few feet under, where the water felt cool against his skin. He made sure no one—especially not Rickenbacker—could see him. He let the salt water flood his mouth. He swallowed, and then he did it again. He knew it wasn't good for him, but he couldn't help himself. He'd been watching Alex drink from the ocean all along. And everyone was getting desperate. They had been more than a week at sea without a drop of freshwater. People had been known to die of dehydration in less time than that.

———◆———

As the sun went down on the eighth night, Rickenbacker felt the temperature drop more than usual. The sky clouded over. The wind picked up, ruffling the surface of the sea. For days the ocean had been calm. Now swells began to lift the rafts and drop them. The familiar roller-coaster ride had begun again—and it meant that rain just might be in the air.

Rickenbacker tried to stay awake. They had a plan for collecting water, and he rehearsed the steps in his mind. But he was so weak that he could feel himself dropping off, his head sinking into Adamson's knees.

At some point in the night, he was jolted awake. The raft had slammed into the bottom of a trough, and all around them the seas were raging. Wind gusted from every direction. The sky had turned a murky gray-black. Every now and then one of the other rafts appeared at the crest of a wave, silhouetted dimly against the sky. The rest of the time, his companions were hidden in the gloom. He could only hope they were still attached.

By midnight, they were all awake and alert, scanning the sky for the telltale vertical streaks of the violent mid-ocean storms known as squalls. At 3 a.m., Rickenbacker heard someone cry out, "Rain!" He lifted his face to the sky, opened his mouth, and felt the drops, cool, clear, and sweet. Then they were gone.

They could see the source of the rain—a fearsome-looking squall hanging in the distance. The men groped for the oars and started paddling. If they could find the strength, and if the wind cooperated, and if they prayed hard enough, they might be able to put themselves in the path of the storm.

It was the clearest sign yet of how desperate they had become. They were eight men jammed into three leaky rafts. Even on the fringes of the squall the sea was lethal. The swells churned and foamed at the crests. Lightning streaked the sky. Claps of thunder rolled across the empty sea. In front of them, all the deadly turmoil of the sky and sea rushed across the horizon in a concentrated column. And they were paddling straight into it, shouting as loud as their dry throats would allow.

The rain came in a curtain, sweeping across the ocean. When it hit them they were ready—underwear, T-shirts, handkerchiefs, socks, and bandages all laid out like washing day on their heads and arms and the sides of the rafts. Water poured from the sky and soaked the garments in seconds. The men wrung the water out furiously and wrung again until the taste of salt was gone. Adamson and Bartek passed clean garments to Rickenbacker, and he started to squeeze the cool freshwater into a bailing bucket.

Just then, he felt a tug at the raft's bowline. He turned in time to see a giant swell turn Whittaker's raft on its side and toss the three men into the ocean. Reynolds! he thought. The radioman couldn't possibly be strong enough to stay afloat in these seas. But the next flash of lightning revealed three men clinging to the handline that ran around the sidewalls of the raft. With Bartek's help, Rickenbacker reeled the raft in and held it tight to their leeward side, sheltering the three men from the waves while they dragged themselves back in.

Cherry, Whittaker, and Reynolds were safe. But what was missing? The Very pistol was gone, along with the rest of the flares and a few cartridges. So was Cherry's bailing bucket and the freshwater he had collected. But the most valuable thing lost was time. They had encountered just one storm in eight days, and it was passing fast.

Rickenbacker went back to work wringing garments into the bucket and watching anxiously for the back edge of the storm. Cherry and Whittaker sucked the water out of their T-shirts and shorts and spit it into the valve of a life vest. Each vest had two inflatable compartments in the chest and another in the neck—enough space to store about a gallon of water. In the doughnut, DeAngelis and Alex had no way to store water, so they collected what they could and wrung it greedily into their mouths.

Then the rain stopped, like someone shutting off a faucet in the sky. What had it been—ten minutes? Twenty? As long as an hour? No one could say.

The important thing was that they now had about a quart and a half of clear, cool, sweet water.

A quart and a half for eight men.

Six ounces of water per person.

Half a glass to keep each man alive until they were lucky enough to drift into another storm.

CHAPTER 10

DESPAIR

They started with an ounce of water on the morning of the ninth day. Rickenbacker poured each ration carefully into one of the remaining Very cartridges and passed it down the line. The handoff from raft to raft was made with great caution. All eyes watched as the man whose turn it was drained the tiny vessel. Even so, as the cartridge made its way back, everyone who handled it brought it to his mouth and lifted his face to the sky, hoping to catch one remaining drop.

———◆———

The excitement of the night before still hung in the air—the mad dash for the storm; the scramble to save Cherry, Whittaker, and Reynolds; the first taste of freshwater in more than a week.

But each ray of hope seemed to dim as soon as it appeared. And like the empty sky after a flare burned through its powder, their prospects for survival looked darker than before.

Rickenbacker carved up the one remaining fish and doled out each portion. Now they had no food and a paltry ration of water to show for their efforts in the night. Despite their initial success using the bird intestines as bait, they hadn't caught another fish since.

One day, Whittaker decided to go shark hunting. He got out the pliers and set to work making a weapon out of an aluminum oar. He bent the corners of the paddle end back and forth until they broke off. After some pains-taking work, he had something resembling a large, clumsy arrowhead at the tip of a spear. He knelt at the side of the raft, waited for a shark to surface within reach, and stabbed at it as hard as he could. The oar bounced harmlessly off the shark's hide. After a few more tries, Whittaker gave up in disgust.

Shortly after they consumed the second fish, Cherry tried to tempt a two-foot shark with an empty hook. To everyone's surprise, the shark bit. Cherry wrestled it onto his lap and stabbed at it with a sheath knife. The shark bucked and writhed, and the raft nearly capsized. Whittaker and Reynolds clung to the side rope. Finally, Cherry drove the knife through the shark's head, and the fight was over.

When they carved the fish up, the meat was so rubbery and foul-tasting that most of the men threw their portions overboard. Cherry, Whittaker, and Reynolds were left with a hole in the floor of their raft where the knife had punctured it during the struggle. They plugged it as best they could with a leftover shell from the .45.

Not long after, a shark carried away the last of their fishhooks.

<hr>

Midway through their second week at sea, a deep gloom settled over the rafts. The eight men had no gear to fish with and no guns to hunt with. They had no flares to signal a passing ship or plane. Everything except Whittaker's watch had stopped working. The compass had frozen in place. Rickenbacker's map was waterlogged and useless. His orders, which he had preserved in his pocket, were unreadable.

As for the rest of humanity, there had been no sign of them since the last radio contact on the afternoon of October 21.

Physically, the raft mates were failing fast. Each of them had lost more than twenty pounds. Reynolds, in particular, had begun to look like a skeleton. He and

Colonel Adamson and Sergeant Alex were so weak they could barely move.

Sun and salt continued to torment them. Bartek's eyes burned from the glare and the salt crust that clung to his eyelashes. His skin became a reddened minefield of salt ulcers. Whittaker escaped the angry sores for some reason, but everyone else was plagued by them. They started as a rash on the thighs and the butt after days of chafing in wet pants. Salt ground its way into the rash, and the ulcers appeared, filled with pus and tender to the touch. Eventually they broke open, leaving wounds that never healed. No one could shift positions without sending a raft mate into an angry tirade.

Whittaker tried to act as peacemaker, but there was no comfort to be found on the rafts. During the day, they lay in a stupor, hiding from the sun and praying for night to fall. At night they huddled together for warmth and wished for day to come. No matter how they arranged themselves in the rafts, there was no relief. Lie back-to-back and the salt spray lashed at your face. Huddle together in the center and you sank into the salt bilge on the floor of the raft.

For Rickenbacker, the nights brought on a loneliness deeper than anything he had felt. The other rafts disappeared in the dark. A groan or a prayer arose from the mist, but he couldn't see anyone. On calm nights, he would awake from a nightmare to find the lines slack and no sound at all in the air. He would sit up and reel in the other rafts until he was sure they were still there.

The men all had good dreams, too, in which giant feasts appeared on their tables at home and they slept peacefully in their own beds. But those were a worse torment than the nightmares, because eventually they woke up. Once Rickenbacker awoke from a fitful sleep and turned to Adamson. "I just telephoned Adelaide, and she's bringing the car right over," he said with a broad grin on his face.

Then he realized where he was.

As the agony mounted, discipline on the rafts started to fall apart. DeAngelis gave up calculating how far they had drifted. Rickenbacker stopped trying to schedule the two-hour night watches. Bartek even freed himself from the constraints of military rank for a while. After all, *Colonel* Rickenbacker drank from the same Very cartridge that *Private* Bartek peed in. Bartek started calling the old man "Rick."

Whether he was the Colonel or just Rick didn't seem

to matter to Rickenbacker. What he cared about was the morale in the rafts—and it was slipping fast. DeAngelis and Reynolds seemed to have given up all hope. From time to time Bartek heard DeAngelis mutter, "Well, I guess tomorrow we'll go to meet our Maker."

The complaints drew the same reaction from Rickenbacker every time: pure, blunt rage. The outbursts were shaped by the world Rickenbacker lived in—a world run by men. In his lifetime, the racetrack, the military, and the top ranks of the business world were mostly male territory. And to Rickenbacker, the important virtues—courage, determination, self-reliance—were *male* virtues. When his raft mates fell short of his standards, he thought they weren't "man enough" for the task at hand.

"What's that?!" he would say at the first sign of moaning. "Why, you damn quitter! When we get out of this, you better crawl home to the women where you belong. How did you get into the army, anyway?!"

On the tenth night, Rickenbacker heard someone praying that God would put him out of his misery.

"He answers MEN'S prayers," the colonel barked out across the waves. "Not that stuff."

To the rest of the men it wasn't clear whether Rickenbacker's outbursts were an act or just plain bullying. The old war hero acted as though he were in charge of the rafts. And when he spoke—or yelled—he did it with such conviction that it was impossible to argue with him.

Rickenbacker's "tongue-lashings," as Bartek called them, did have one effect. In the moment, they made each crew member in his turn hate the old man with a passion. And hatred, at least, was more likely to keep a man alive than despair.

Often, after tempers settled down, the men felt reflective. When you were in the middle of life—following orders, getting up for work every day—it was easy to take it all for granted. You assumed that your friends and family would be there forever, so they didn't need special attention. What you did or failed to do each day didn't matter all that much; there was always another day.

But out here, drifting 500 miles from nowhere, you saw life for what it really was: fragile as an egg. One miscalculation—a broken octant or a faulty wind-speed reading—and it could all be stolen away.

So in the relative comfort of dawn and dusk, they talked about their lives. They confessed sins from the past and resolved to do better in the future. Life, after all, was not to be wasted—if they ever got a second chance.

DeAngelis felt bad that he hadn't bothered to do anything special with his wife after they got married. If he made it back, he pledged, he would take her to all the best nightclubs.

Adamson talked about the homeless people he used to see on the streets of New York City—people who didn't have enough to eat. He vowed that if he survived, he'd do something to help them. He'd always thought he was so "big" and important back at home. Out here, he realized it was all false pride. He passed around a picture of his wife and asked the rest of the crew to make sure they gave it to her if he didn't make it back.

Whittaker admitted that he'd been selfish all his life. He was way too quick to get into arguments and not quick enough to make up. He had a brother he hadn't spoken to in fifteen years. If he made it back he was going to get in touch with him and apologize.

Cherry confessed that he had a girlfriend in Australia whom he had met on an Air Transport mission. She looked just like the actress Olivia de Havilland, he said. But now his family at home was all he could think about—especially his little daughter, Paula. He had missed important parts of her life, and if he ever got back to Texas, she was going to be his priority.

At some point Sergeant Alex revealed to DeAngelis that before they left Hawaii, he had written a month's worth of letters to his girlfriend, Snooks. He had given them to a friend with instructions to mail one a day.

———◆———

While Alex daydreamed about Snooks, everyone else began to wonder how much longer he could last. By the tenth day, he thrashed miserably in the tiny doughnut, and DeAngelis struggled to keep him from plunging into the sea. His head burned with fever. He muttered and moaned and didn't seem to recognize anyone. They increased his ration of water, but it didn't seem to help.

Finally, Rickenbacker suggested they move him into one of the bigger rafts. They pulled the doughnut close and DeAngelis, Bartek, and Rickenbacker struggled to get Alex over the sidewalls and into Rickenbacker's raft. Bartek climbed awkwardly into the doughnut and pretzeled himself in with DeAngelis.

Rickenbacker arranged Alex low in the raft and positioned himself to block the wind. He lay close and cradled him like a baby to help transfer body heat. Alex shivered uncontrollably and mumbled in a language that sounded to Rickenbacker like Polish. In about an hour, he relaxed and dropped into a fitful sleep.

CHAPTER 11

LETTERS TO SNOOKS

"Army planes en route to the Southwest Pacific have joined the search for Captain E.V. ('Eddie') Rickenbacker, War Department officials disclosed today, in the hope that the missing World War I ace might still be found."

That was the news from Washington, D.C., on November 1, the twelfth day since the world had last heard from the B-17 crew. Unlike many newspaper editors, the U.S. military had not given up on the lost men. Planes headed for the battlefront in the Solomon Islands were to break formation and fan out to look for a stray raft on the waves below.

To the fliers peering out the windows of their warplanes, finding Eddie Rickenbacker was probably not the foremost thing on their minds. They were headed back into some of the most brutal fighting of the war.

Four of them had been trotted out to talk to reporters

at Hickam Field just two days earlier. They had been on Guadalcanal, the tiny jungle island that figured heavily in Rickenbacker's mission. Since October 12, the Japanese had been trying desperately to win back the island's airstrip. It was "the site of a life-and-death struggle," reported the *New York Times*. The outcome could decide the war in the Pacific for good.

A Life-and-Death Struggle: U.S. infantrymen on Guadalcanal regroup after defending a peak called the Grassy Knoll from a Japanese attack.

According to what the fliers told reporters, they had some things in common with the castaways on the rafts.

They barely slept, thanks to relentless bombing runs by the Japanese. By 11 p.m. every night they were up and running for their foxholes. "The ground was shaking all the time like jelly," said one of the men. They were also hungry most of the time, because Japanese warships surrounding the island made it hard for the Americans to land supplies. The men were stuck with two small meals a day—mostly rice left behind by the Japanese.

On October 24, about the time Rickenbacker had been scheduled to arrive in the area, the marines held off a massive attack by the Japanese on the outskirts of the airstrip. The fighting left a line of Japanese corpses stretching for half a mile along the edge of the jungle. It also left the Americans with fewer than thirty planes to fend off the bombings. Japanese ships were still massing in the waters around Guadalcanal. It was obvious they were preparing to land another wave of troops. The marines needed planes fast from bases in Hawaii and the mainland United States, and that meant that more pilots were in the sky with orders to look for eight men that most Americans had already given up on.

⸻◈⸻

On the rafts, the men almost never mentioned the war. Rickenbacker was determined to get back and complete his mission, but he kept his thoughts to himself. The rest of the men had no idea what was happening in Guadalcanal or the Soviet Union or North Africa. Nor did they care. The newspapers and the generals and the politicians claimed they were fighting for freedom and democracy. But in the rafts, the men found it hard to get excited about noble causes when they'd had six ounces of water to drink in two weeks. DeAngelis, for one, was bitter that he had to die of dehydration "all because some guys made up their minds to have a war."

Of the eight raft mates, however, DeAngelis was not the one closest to death.

———●———

When the sun rose on their twelfth day at sea, everyone was relieved to see that Alex's condition had improved. He seemed to know where he was and who his raft mates were. As the day wore on, though, he sank into a familiar state. His forehead felt hot as the sun. When he tried to talk he made no sense.

Alex rallied again as the air cooled, and that evening he asked to go back to the small raft. This time, DeAngelis traded places with Alex. Bartek took his fellow engineer into the doughnut and tried to get comfortable. But Alex would not sit still. He squirmed and draped himself over the side of the raft. Bartek quickly realized he was trying to end it all by giving himself up to the ocean.

Bartek maneuvered Alex's legs under his and sat on them. When the wretched kid complained, Bartek let him squat on the floor of the raft. He spread his own legs out on the sidewalls so Alex would have to climb over them to get out. At one point during the night he had to grab Alex just before he slipped into the ocean.

In the darkness, Bartek could hear his raft mate mumbling to no one in particular. For several days, Alex hadn't spoken much at all. Now he sounded more coherent than he had the entire trip. He prayed that he would see his mother; his sister; and his girlfriend, Snooks, again. Somewhere around two or three in the morning, he mumbled what sounded like a familiar prayer:

"Holy Mother Mary. Mary Mother of God, pray for us."

He ended with an "Amen."

And then he stopped moving.

Bartek knew what had happened, but he willed himself to check. In the darkness, he found Alex's arm and felt for a pulse.

Nothing.

He leaned forward and put his hand over Alex's heart.

Nothing.

Twenty feet away in the middle raft, Rickenbacker woke up. He thought he heard a long sigh. Maybe Bartek had called to him and he heard the words in a half-conscious state. Maybe he simply knew.

"Did he die?" he called out across the waves.

"I think so," Bartek said.

They pulled the rafts close. Rickenbacker, Cherry, and Whittaker examined Alex as well as they could in the dark. There was no question he was dead, but they agreed they should wait till first light to do anything else.

"Well," someone said, "his sufferings are over."

They let the rafts drift apart. The wind had come up strong, and the sea churned around them. Rickenbacker had heard that sharks can sense death even before it arrives. He thought the fins around the rafts had already multiplied.

The predators circled in the dark. Clouds raced across the sky in the moonlight. The familiar loneliness of night set in, and this time it was accompanied by fear.

In the doughnut, Bartek began the long wait till morning with Alex's legs slowly stiffening in his lap.

In Connecticut, Coreen Bond, known as "Snooks" to her boyfriend, had already woken up to a Monday morning. Before long, she would be checking her mailbox to find yet another letter, postmarked "Hawaii" and signed by Alex Kaczmarczyk.

CHAPTER 12

DAYDREAMS

On the morning of November 2, the thirteenth day at sea, they brought the rafts close again and dug in Alex's pockets for his wallet. They took his identification tag from around his neck. Cherry held on to both in the hope that he would be able to return them to Alex's family. Bartek asked if he could have Alex's leather jacket to help keep him warm at night. Rigor mortis had set in, and Alex's limbs were rigid. It took Bartek several minutes to wrestle the jacket free of the body.

No one discussed the prospect of using the corpse for food.

DeAngelis murmured what he remembered of the Catholic burial service. "I consign your body to the sea and your soul to the Lord," he said in conclusion.

Then they rolled Alex's body over the side and into the ocean. He floated facedown for some time before the men lost sight of him.

Burial at Sea: Two navy men killed in battle get a formal ceremony near the Gilbert Islands, later in the war.

With Alex gone, a new kind of gloom settled over the rafts. For two weeks, they had imagined their own deaths. Now the prospect was real. Alex had been the weakest of the group from the start, but could the rest of them be far behind? Reynolds had probably lost a third of his body weight and looked more dead than alive. Bartek was a skeletal mass of salt ulcers and roasted skin. Rickenbacker seemed to be running on bile alone.

DeAngelis was in better shape than everyone except Whittaker and Cherry, but he took Alex's death especially hard. He had only known the kid for two weeks, but he'd spent the better part of that time virtually sitting in his lap and watching while he wasted away. Now DeAngelis lost all faith in their chances—and that made him a terrible raft mate for Rickenbacker. The two of them started arguing almost as soon as DeAngelis climbed in, and DeAngelis didn't have the patience for it. He asked to trade places with Reynolds. If it was all going to end soon, he wanted to be with his captain, Bill Cherry.

———◆———

Around the fourteenth day, another storm overtook them, and they collected water with practiced skill. Rickenbacker transferred their hoard in his mouth from bucket to vest, and he could feel his raft mates watching to make sure he didn't swallow. Someone grumbled that the process was taking way too long.

After the storm, the weather grew dead calm.

When DeAngelis joined Cherry and Whittaker, it put the three strongest men in one raft. That gave Cherry an idea: He and his raft mates, he announced, were going to cut loose from the others. The current, at this point, seemed to be pushing them steadily north. If the three of them put all their remaining strength into the oars, they might be able to get back on a southwest course. And that would carry them away from the Japanese, toward the Ellice Islands, Fiji, and survival. In any case, Cherry insisted, spreading out would give the search planes—assuming they were still up there—a better chance of finding them.

Rickenbacker was furious. Their best hope lay in staying together, he was convinced of it. They'd be easier to see from the sky. They needed one another for support. And besides, without Cherry and Whittaker, no one had the strength to pull a man back in the raft if someone went overboard.

When Cherry refused to bend, Rickenbacker tried to pull rank. "I forbid you to go," he said.

"Under what circumstances?" Cherry said.

"I'm a colonel," Rickenbacker shot back. "I'm ordering you not to go."

Cherry and Whittaker reminded Rickenbacker that his rank made no difference, because he wasn't in the army. He was a civilian acting under orders from the secretary of war.

Adamson mustered enough strength to insist that he was an acting colonel, which put him in charge. He was ordering them not to go.

"I am in charge of the airplane," Cherry shot back. "That means I'm in charge of this trip until we get back to land."

The entire argument seemed ridiculous to DeAngelis. They weren't getting back to land—not now, not tomorrow, not next week. Rickenbacker and Adamson were fighting with their last ounces of strength to call themselves captains of a sinking ship.

Rickenbacker finally gave in and watched while Cherry, Whittaker, and DeAngelis drifted into the distance. The three men pointed themselves toward the southwest and took turns with the oars, two people rowing while one rested. Several hours later, they were still visible, maybe a mile away.

Exhausted from the effort, all three men fell sound asleep. When they awoke, they paddled slowly back and tied onto the other two rafts. The argument, and the effort, had all come to nothing.

In the brutal calm, time slipped past like the sea, with no milestone or benchmark. There was only the relentless cycle of blinding sun and terrifying darkness, scorching heat and bone-chilling cold.

Simple tasks now required superhuman effort. Blowing up the sidewalls of a raft now took two of them more than two hours. Every now and then, they would try again to paddle toward the southwest. No one had the strength to keep at it. After a few minutes they would collapse against the sides of the rafts and give in to the still water.

Occasionally, they stumbled onto a paltry ration of food. At one point, two silvery fish jumped into one of the rafts to escape a shark, and the men were on them in seconds. On another day, thousands of fingerlings—juvenile fish the size of a finger—swept past the boat in sheets. The water was so dense with fish that the men were able to grab a few with their bare hands. The unlucky fingerlings were swallowed whole while they were still alive.

After the last storm, they had nearly a gallon of water stored in the life vests. It felt good to have a reserve, but they still doled it out in 1- or 2-ounce portions twice a day. The tiny amount barely freed the tongue from the roof of the mouth for a few minutes. It was nowhere near enough to stave off the ravages of dehydration.

Under normal conditions, blood feeds the brain with the oxygen it needs to function. Now, with such a paltry supply of water, the amount of blood in each man's body dwindled. Their veins shrank, and their brains began to starve for oxygen.

Dehydration sent the men into bouts of delirium. Day and night, they drifted in and out of a dream state, the line between sleep and wakefulness vanishing fast. Hallucinations crept into the hours when they were fully awake.

One night, before he moved into Rickenbacker's boat, Reynolds sat up and whispered to Whittaker: "Say, I guess you know about DeAngelis and Cherry. They land on a secret island and get themselves a quart of water and then they come back and sit in the boat again. Shhhh, don't let the captain hear that."

Rickenbacker woke up in a stupor and overheard Reynolds. "Well, I'll be damned!" Rickenbacker yelled. "If anybody has an island, they better take me!"

Every night, Rickenbacker had his own island dreams. Usually, they just happened to land in a place where an old friend had a beautiful house. The friend took him in, gave him a comfortable bed, and served him fruit juice. In the morning all he'd have to do is wake up, reach for the phone, and call Secretary of War Stimson, who would dispatch a plane to fly him home to Adelaide.

Instead he woke up in three inches of salt water, wedged between two starving men and floating in the middle of the Pacific.

Bartek thought he was truly going crazy. The clouds transformed into people and animals, hovering over the raft: a chicken, a giant bird, a woman with a dog in her lap. Under the menagerie, he drifted in and out of day-dreams. In the strange space between asleep and awake, Bartek's family visited him in the raft. His mother appeared and told him he would have to rely on God. His sister Ruth, who had died six weeks ago, told him she was okay and he would be, too.

CHAPTER 13

CONTACT

The eighteenth day dawned in a furnace. Jim Whittaker cursed out loud at the sun before it appeared above the horizon. He had grown to hate the sun and the sea as though they had made a conscious choice to torture him.

The flare cartridge made its way around to him with the morning's ration—a paltry inch of piss-warm water in the bottom. It tasted awful and only served to remind him how thirsty he was.

By noon, the daily chorus of delirium rose from the rafts. There was random shouting in parched voices. Someone sang a line of an unrecognizable song before trailing off. Everyone took turns talking to people who weren't there.

Whittaker had been carrying on a running conversation with Davy Jones, the mythical evil spirit of the sea. Today, he heard a new voice—one that left him shaken and scared. It was his son, Tom; he was sure of it. Tom had been training for the navy in California when they left two and half weeks ago.

"What are you doing out here, Tom?" he asked, speaking into the air. "When did you leave San Francisco?"

His son's voice replied: "I was sent to sea over two weeks ago, Dad. You see—we were sunk. And seeing I was out here I thought I'd just drop in and see how you are getting along."

Whittaker called out to him and called out again, but the voice was gone. He settled back into the raft, wondering if his son could be dead and speaking to him from beyond the grave.

He was still agonizing over the thought when he saw Bill Cherry sit up straight in the raft. Cherry's eyes looked wild in their bony sockets.

"I hear an engine!" he yelled. "Hear it?!"

Whittaker looked around at the gaunt faces of his raft mates. No one, with the possible exception of Rickenbacker, believed it was anything but a hallucination.

Another moment passed in silence. Suddenly, seven men sat bolt upright, staring into the sky. There was no mistaking it—a low, muffled roar in the distance, unlike any sound made by the sea or sky. Cherry and Rickenbacker saw the plane first, emerging from a cloud bank about five

Contact: An OS2U Kingfisher on patrol for the navy.

miles to the west. It looked like it was headed straight for the rafts.

Bartek thought it was American—a navy Kingfisher with pontoons and a single engine. But at this point, no one cared if it was Emperor Tojo of Japan himself. They yelled as loud as they could. Cherry flapped his undershirt sail in the air. Bartek somehow found the strength to stand. He waved his arms wildly while Rickenbacker held him by the waist.

Whittaker's first instinct was to reach for the flares. Then he realized they were long gone. In the next instant he knew that without them, the rafts were completely invisible to a plane that far away.

The plane teased them for a couple of minutes before disappearing into the clouds three miles off. The promising hum of the engine faded seconds later, and with it went every shred of hope. The men collapsed, exhausted from the effort. They sat in silence, throats burning, spirits crushed.

They had been out here eighteen days without a single sign that other people inhabited the globe. Now a pilot had entered their world—and left just as quickly, with no idea they existed. How could they possibly make it till they got another chance? DeAngelis and Bartek had been drinking salt water, just like Alex had before he died. Reynolds was a human skeleton; he looked like he wouldn't make it another day. It felt to Whittaker like the cruelest moment of the whole ordeal—to have the promise of rescue dangled nearly within reach, and then snatched away.

Rickenbacker let them stew in despair for a few minutes while he gathered his strength. Then he launched into another lecture. That plane, he said, meant they had drifted within range of a base. If that was true, they were moving in the right direction and would keep drifting closer. That meant there would be more planes and more chances to be seen. "A *man*," he told the crew, would have the courage, the patience, and the faith to swallow his disappointment, hang on, and wait.

And so they did.

The next morning, another plane appeared, and yet another in the afternoon. Each time the scene from the day before repeated itself. Stick-figure arms waved in the air. Ruined voices shouted into the sky. The plane disappeared. The men collapsed. Rickenbacker growled at his raft mates until they wanted to survive, if for no other reason than to see him put in his grave.

The following day—their twentieth at sea—Rickenbacker was sitting listlessly in the sun when he heard voices arguing. DeAngelis was now alone in the small raft, and Cherry was asking him to trade places.

"Why?" DeAngelis asked.

"I'm going to try to make land," Cherry said. "Staying together's no good. They'll never see us this way."

Rickenbacker couldn't believe Cherry wanted to go off on his own again. It had been two days since they first saw the planes, and the men felt like time was running out. But splitting up could mean death for all of them, and Rickenbacker let Cherry know it. If the planes couldn't see all three rafts bunched together, how were they going to catch sight of one? And how would Cherry know which way to row? The planes had come from all directions of the compass. There was land somewhere nearby, but no one knew where it was.

Cherry and Rickenbacker argued back and forth, locked in another power struggle. Finally Cherry put an end to it. "I was captain and commanding officer of the plane," he insisted. "I am the commanding officer of this party. I'm leaving."

DeAngelis paddled up to Cherry's raft. The two men switched places, and Cherry rowed off in the doughnut. The rest of the crew watched as their captain drifted away on the waves.

The copilot and the navigator weren't far behind. Before Cherry disappeared over the horizon, Whittaker and DeAngelis announced that they were leaving, too.

Rickenbacker was furious now. He did not want to be left alone with Adamson and Bartek, both of whom were so weak they could barely lift their heads. "What about Reynolds?" he said. "You haven't asked him."

Reynolds was too far gone to ask.

Whittaker didn't bother to argue with Rickenbacker. He untied his line and dropped it in the ocean. The three rafts, together for nearly three weeks, gradually drifted apart.

CHAPTER 14

RACE AGAINST TIME

Jim Whittaker finally fell asleep just before dawn the next morning. It had been a fitful night, not because of the pain or the miserable jumble of legs and arms in the raft. For once, he was excited. Yesterday, he had seen the evening patrol pass closer than it had the last three days. The rafts had drifted two, maybe three miles apart. Surely this time the Kingfisher had flown right over one of them. Whittaker was convinced that something good was about to happen.

He hadn't been asleep long when he felt DeAngelis shaking him by the shoulder and yelling his name.

Whittaker was groggy from lack of sleep. "Cut that out!" he croaked. "What's the matter with you!"

"Jim, you'd better take a look," DeAngelis said. "It may be a mirage, but I think I see something."

Whittaker propped himself up in the raft and looked toward the horizon. It was no mirage. Ten or twelve miles out, the line where the sea met the sky bristled with the faint outline of trees.

The sight was more than enough to rouse Whittaker. He set the oars, gathered his strength, and started rowing. DeAngelis took over from time to time, but he could only pull for a few minutes before collapsing.

Reynolds lay behind Whittaker, too weak to sit up all the way. "I feel all right," he would say. "Just tired. I'll get up in a minute and help you, Jim." When the sun rose high, he filled flare cartridges with seawater and poured them over Whittaker's head.

Seven and a half hours later, they fought their way through a riptide and a storm and eased themselves over a shallow reef. DeAngelis lay across the bow, guiding the raft with his hands so it didn't rip on the sharp coral. Finally, they ran aground forty feet from shore.

They had been at sea for twenty-one days—three weeks of constant motion. And now they had come to rest. They had each at various times given up all hope of seeing land again, all hope of hugging friends and family, all hope of living to see their grandchildren. Now they had found their way back—to somewhere, anyway.

One by one they tried to stand up in the shallow water. The island tilted and swayed under their feet, as though they were still at sea. All three of them collapsed to their knees. Reynolds could not get up. He crawled toward the beach. Whittaker and DeAngelis each leaned on an oar and hobbled like old men to shore.

———◆———

At 3:45 that afternoon, on the island of Funafuti, Radioman Second Class Lester Boutte took his seat in the rear of an OS2U Kingfisher seaplane. The plane was an awkward-looking thing, with a bloated cigar of a pontoon suspended from the middle of the fuselage. Boutte's pilot, Lieutenant Frederick Woodward, taxied toward the middle

The Kingfisher flew scouting missions for the navy. It could take off and land at sea.

of Funafuti's Te Namo lagoon and opened the throttle. The plane picked up speed, skidded across the salt water, and lifted into the air.

It was just another evening patrol for Boutte and Woodward. The marines had occupied Funafuti six weeks ago, and they'd been flying patrols ever since. The Japanese base in the Gilberts lay 500 miles north. The idea was to keep the enemy from moving south to threaten the shipping route to Australia. From the air over Funafuti, you could already see antiaircraft guns guarding the beach, giant searchlights marking both ends of the island, an airfield taking shape among the palm trees.

Woodward and Boutte started their usual circuit, looking for signs of Japanese planes, ships, or subs. Fifty minutes into the patrol, Boutte spotted a speck of yellow on the waves below. Woodward banked and dropped low over the water. The two fliers got close enough to make out an emaciated man with rags for clothes. Boutte's pulse quickened. What else could the ragged figure be but a survivor from the lost B-17 that had gone down with Eddie Rickenbacker aboard?

All American forces in the area were operating under strict radio silence to keep Japanese intelligence in the dark. But Woodward and Boutte sped back to Funafuti and dropped a message to their commander. The commander dispatched a PT (Patrol Torpedo) boat with orders to rush to the area, find the survivor, and pick him up.

By 9:30 p.m., Captain Bill Cherry had been lifted from the doughnut by the crew of the PT boat and was sitting aboard the USS *Hilo*. His body was covered in salt-water ulcers. His skin was red and raw to the touch. He weighed 45 pounds less than he did when he left Hickam Field three weeks earlier. But he was healthy enough to tell his rescuers that there were two more rafts floating not far from where he was found. In them were six more men, each of them alive—for now.

———●———

Whittaker, DeAngelis, and Reynolds slept that night on land with the raft over them for shelter. They had made their way to the other side of the island, where the trees blocked the wind and sun. They seemed to have landed at the very end of a peninsula, where the island was only a few hundred yards across. So far there were no signs of other inhabitants, American or Japanese.

On the way across the island they collected coconuts that had fallen to the ground, but they were so weak it took them forty minutes to cut through a single shell. When they set up camp, a swarm of rodents came to investigate. Whittaker managed to club two of them to death. Then he went back to the beach, where pockets of coral poked above the surface of the ocean. Rainwater had puddled in the coral, and he painstakingly filled a life vest. He brought his stash back to the men. They feasted on dry, overripe coconut pulp, raw rodent meat, and freshwater.

After the meal, Reynolds only looked worse. His eyes had sunk a half-inch into his skull. He had gone from 130 to about 90 pounds. If they didn't find help soon, he wasn't going to make it.

When they lay down and pulled the raft over them, the ground seemed to sway more violently than the ocean had on their worst nights at sea.

———◈———

The next morning, at first light, all five Kingfisher seaplanes based on Funafuti took to the air. Four PT boats fanned out across the sea. The planes flew in formation, searching area A, one of three zones they had mapped out the night before. By mid-morning they had found nothing.

The planes refueled, then split into two groups and searched areas B and C. Still nothing.

An emergency signal came in from Nukufetau, an island 60 miles northwest of Funafuti. It turned out to be nothing, too.

By mid-afternoon, the Kingfishers had covered the

areas they intended to search and were running low on fuel. It wouldn't be long before darkness shut down any hope of spotting the survivors.

The fliers headed back toward Funafuti, scanning waters they had already searched, just in case.

———◆———

That same morning, November 12, Rickenbacker was beginning to lose hope. He and Bartek and Adamson hadn't seen a plane since the rafts split up. He had a strong suspicion they had traveled right through a chain of islands and were drifting out to sea again.

His hand shook as he poured the morning's ration of water. Adamson and Bartek could barely raise their heads to drink.

"Have the planes come back?" Bartek mumbled.

"No," Rickenbacker said.

"They won't come back," Bartek said. "I know they won't come back."

Again and again he repeated it, until he lapsed into a stupor.

Rickenbacker passed the time dangling his hands in the water, trying to grab fingerlings as they skittered past. He got a couple, but his hands didn't seem to be taking signals from his brain properly.

He was half conscious under the afternoon sun when he felt Bartek tugging at his shirt.

"Listen, Captain," he said. "Planes! They're back!"

Rickenbacker looked up to see two planes fly within a couple of miles of the raft, only to vanish into the clouds.

Then, a half hour later, two more appeared in the west. This time they kept coming, directly at the tiny raft. At this point, none of the men were strong enough to stand up. Instead, they sat as tall as they could, waving shirts and hats, yelling till they went hoarse.

The planes came closer and closer until one broke formation and angled down. It banked and began to circle the raft from a few hundred feet away, its bulbous pontoon just a hundred feet off the water. A radioman sat in the rear seat, smiling and waving at the men in the raft. Rickenbacker kept waving back long after it was clear they had been seen. He couldn't quite convince himself that the fliers knew they were not three dead men in a raft.

Yet there was no question about it. For the first time in more than three weeks, someone knew they were alive.

But the pilot kept circling. In a little while, another pilot came to relieve him. The sun sank deeper in the west, and Rickenbacker wondered why they didn't land. Maybe the pilots had called for a PT boat to come pick them up.

But once darkness fell the plane would return to base. There was no way a boat would be able to find them in the dark. And they could drift 10, maybe 20 miles overnight. Wasn't it possible they would be lost again—this time for good?

———◆———

By late afternoon, the Kingfisher squadron on Funafuti could congratulate themselves: They had found Rickenbacker. Now they had to get him home.

For Lieutenant William Eadie, commander of the squadron, that was a problem. Landing a Kingfisher in mid-ocean was no easy task. And even if a pilot landed safely, how would he transport three passengers in a plane designed for two people? He would have no chance of taking off with the extra weight.

The force commander on Funafuti broke radio silence at 5:40 p.m. for the first time since marines arrived on the island. He radioed coordinates for Rickenbacker's raft to the four PT boats. But the nearest boat was at least five hours from the raft. It would be pitch-dark by the time it arrived.

When the news came in from the PT boats, Eadie made a decision. With radioman Lester Boutte in the rear, he would take off for Rickenbacker's raft and try to pick up the survivors himself.

At some point that afternoon, Jim Whittaker had been standing on the beach staring out at the ocean. It was hard to tell in the sunlit glare, but it looked like a squadron of ships was headed for the island—destroyers, maybe.

He shook DeAngelis awake. They had gone back in the raft that morning and rowed south along the shore until they found a small hut on the beach. It was a modest thing, but it was the first sign of civilization they had seen in three weeks. To Whittaker it might as well have been New York City. They had found fresh rainwater in some broken coconut shells, and then went back to sleep.

DeAngelis sat up when Whittaker shook him, then looked out at the water.

"They're just barges," he mumbled, and lay back down to close his eyes again.

"Just barges!" Whittaker yelled. "What do you want, the *Queen Mary*?!"

Whittaker scrambled to the raft and rowed out to meet the squadron. As it drew closer, the sun's glare lifted, and what Whittaker had thought to be "destroyers" were revealed to be outrigger canoes crewed by islanders. The men in the lead boat welcomed Whittaker to their home by tying his raft to their boat. They sped to shore, and a young man jumped out with a crude machete and a length of rope. He wrapped the rope around a coconut tree and scrambled up with ease. By the time Whittaker arrived at the hut with the rest of the outrigger crew, there was fresh coconut milk waiting. He and DeAngelis and Reynolds drank it in. The islanders helped them aboard the canoe and sped off around the coast of the island.

By evening, they sat in a village of small huts with thatched palm fronds for roofs. The smell of chicken soup hung in the air. Their rescuers were residents of Nukufetau and were already hosting a wireless station manned by Allied intelligence officers from New Zealand. Earlier that day, a plane from Funafuti had dropped a message asking the station to be on the lookout for survivors from the B-17.

The villagers welcomed Whittaker and his ragged companions with open arms. Some of them wept openly when they saw how emaciated the men were. A nineteen-year-old islander named Toma presented Whittaker with a miniature model of the canoe he had been rescued in. "Jim America," Toma called him.

Two New Zealanders from the wireless station soon arrived with the news that they had radioed Funafuti. The officers poured fruit juice for the survivors, and for once, Whittaker could watch the sunset without it tormenting him.

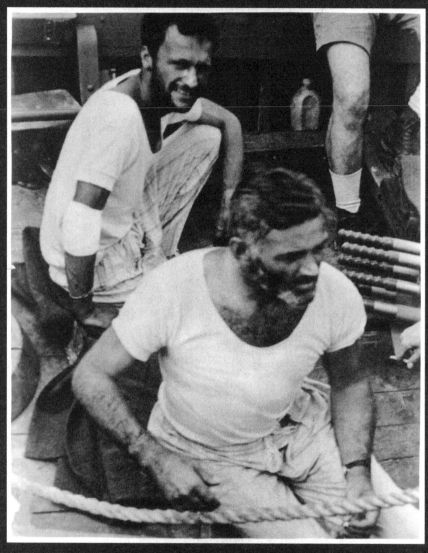

Survivors: DeAngelis (rear) and Whittaker, back on land after 22 days at sea.

Just before dark, a navy Kingfisher from Funafuti taxied into the lagoon. A military doctor jumped from its rear seat and hurried ashore. With him were the glucose injections that would finally give Jim Reynolds's starved body the fuel it needed to survive.

While Whittaker, DeAngelis, and Reynolds filled themselves with chicken soup, Rickenbacker floated miles away, fretting. He watched the sun disappear over the horizon with dread. A Kingfisher still circled overhead. But a dark squall hung over the southern sky. If they weren't picked up tonight and that squall caught them, who knew how far it would blow them.

As the last bit of light faded, a blinding white flare lit the sky beneath the Kingfisher. A minute later, the plane shot another flare, this one red. In the eerie glow, the pilot angled down, knifed his pontoon into the water, and settled into a smooth landing. He taxied to the raft and shut his engine down. Rickenbacker rowed close enough to grab the pontoon.

The man in the rear seat climbed onto the wing and introduced himself: Radioman Lester Boutte. The pilot was Lieutenant William Eadie. To Rickenbacker, who had lost 40 pounds, the men looked like the strongest, healthiest human beings he had ever seen.

Boutte and Eadie lifted Adamson 8 feet into the rear seat of the plane. A PT boat was on its way, Eadie said, but he didn't want to fire another flare for fear there were Japanese in the area. Without the light, there was no guarantee the PT boat would find them. They weren't going to wait. He and Boutte hoisted Bartek onto the right wing and Rickenbacker onto the left. Boutte tied them to each other and ran the line through the cockpit. Eadie fired up the engine and they started to taxi across the ocean toward Funafuti, 40 miles away.

They hadn't gone more than a few miles when the dark outline of a PT boat appeared in front of them. Minutes later, Rickenbacker sat aboard the boat, sipping beef broth and pineapple juice. Bartek lay exhausted on a mat in the cabin. The boat captain led the Kingfisher, with Adamson still aboard, back to Funafuti.

For three weeks the seven survivors had not been forty feet apart. They shared water parceled out by the ounce and food that might have amounted to one decent meal. Now they were scattered among two islands, a boat, and a plane. Two of them—Adamson and Reynolds—were

Rickenbacker is helped ashore at Funafuti, 40 pounds lighter and shaky on his feet but happy to be alive.

clinging to life. Alex had been lost to the sea. But the rest had survived, and when the next night came they would all be sleeping in beds.

Rickenbacker, it turned out, had been lucky once again.

Just before dawn on the morning of November 13, he and Bartek and Adamson were carried ashore on stretchers. Lying on his back, Rickenbacker watched the moon glimmer through the palm trees. It was, he thought, one of the most beautiful things he had ever seen.

CHAPTER 15

THE ONES NOT TAKEN

News of the rescue traveled fast, from Funafuti to Hawaii to Washington, D.C.

Bill Cherry's wife was the first to find out. She got a phone call at the aircraft factory in Dallas, where she worked. It was Friday the thirteenth. "It must be my luckiest day," she said.

Adelaide Rickenbacker was in her New York City apartment the next morning when General Hap Arnold called. "I have good news for you," he said.

She went on the radio Sunday with a message for all the other mothers and wives who were waiting for news from the front: "Never, never give up hope."

Johnny Bartek's mother, Mary, claimed she had never given up on her son. Then she told a reporter, "It's still hard to believe."

Newspaper reporters all across the country got on the

phone and knocked on doors, looking for reactions to the rescue.

"Swell!" said New York City mayor Fiorello La Guardia, when he heard Rickenbacker was alive.

"Thank God!" said Jack Glynn, a retired morgue keeper interviewed by a New York reporter. "He's damn lucky. He's got more lives than a cat."

"He must have a rabbit's foot or something," said Eddie's brother William.

———◆———

Millions of people soaked up news of the rescue that weekend. There wasn't a lot of detail yet, but most of the commentators didn't care. If you believed the newspapers, this survival story wasn't just about seven men; it was a triumph for a nation at war.

Rickenbacker and the crew showed that "American men have the courage and resourcefulness it takes to come through harrowing ordeals—and win wars," said the *Minneapolis Evening Star.*

The fact that Americans hadn't given up the search proved to a Memphis, Tennessee, newspaper that "we are not a people who hold life cheaply."

The rescue demonstrated the U.S. military's "increasing mastery of the air and sea," according to the *Everett Herald* in Washington. If American planes could pluck three tiny rafts from such a vast stretch of ocean, how could the Japanese or the Germans or the Italians possibly hide from us?

Of course, Rickenbacker, Whittaker, Bartek, and the rest hadn't read the papers yet. They were just seven men, lying in a makeshift hospital in the middle of the Pacific, relieved to be alive. Little did they know they had become

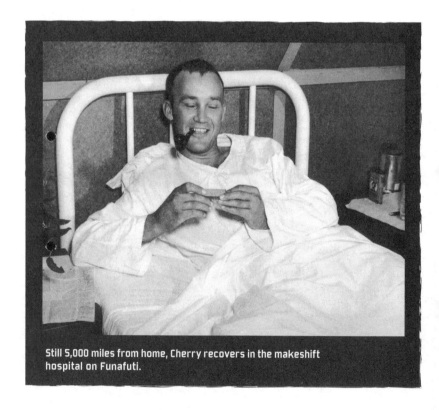

Still 5,000 miles from home, Cherry recovers in the makeshift hospital on Funafuti.

a sign that millions of American soldiers were not risking their lives in vain.

———◆———

On December 10, Eddie Rickenbacker peered out the window of a B-17. This time, he was not lost. A few hundred feet below lay the thick jungle of Guadalcanal. A month ago, Rickenbacker was nearly dead from thirst and starvation. Now he was back at work.

After their rescue, the men had been reunited in Funafuti. Whittaker had weathered the ordeal better than the rest. He walked into the one-room hospital under his own power and saw a shrunken Rickenbacker lying in bed.

"What's the matter, Rick?" he said with a grin. "Been sick?"

After regaining some strength in Funafuti, the survivors flew to Samoa, where they spent a couple of weeks recovering at a hospital. Then Whittaker, Cherry, DeAngelis, and Bartek flew home to Hawaii. Adamson and Reynolds stayed in Samoa for treatment.

Rickenbacker took off for the western Pacific. He had lost a couple dozen pounds, but he was still the man he had been on October 21, when he insisted the crew take off in an uninspected plane. He was determined to complete his mission.

Guadalcanal was the last stop, and as his B-17 touched down, he could already tell it was, in his words, "a hellhole." The landing strip was nothing but a scar in the jungle. On either side, the ground was littered with the twisted wreckage of planes. Pilots called it "the graveyard."

The Graveyard: The remains of an SBD dive bomber litter the forest on Guadalcanal after being shot down by Japanese planes.

Rickenbacker was deeply disturbed by conditions on the island. The rainy season had just started, and there was mud everywhere. Daily bombings ripped holes in the airfield and the tents that housed the marines. When the men scrambled to save themselves from the bombs, they landed in foxholes waist-deep in water. Mosquitos came in swarms. Malaria, dysentery, and meager food rations left everyone weak and feverish. "Everything," the colonel reported, "seems to rot away in the damp."

While Rickenbacker had been out on the rafts, the marines at the airfield and the Japanese soldiers trying to take it back had also been fighting for their lives. By December it looked like the marines had won the advantage. Most likely, Guadalcanal was in American hands for good. But both sides had paid a heavy price: Nearly 40,000 men would die before the end of the campaign.

After one anxious night on the island, Rickenbacker took off on the final leg of his trip. Had he scanned the waters below, about 40 miles off the southern tip of Guadalcanal, he might have seen stray wreckage from a cruiser called the USS *Juneau*. The *Juneau* was one of about 60 ships destroyed in the six-month battle for the island. It was hit by a torpedo on November 13, about twenty-four hours after Rickenbacker was plucked from the sea by William Eadie's seaplane. The torpedo hit the *Juneau*'s ammunition stores, and a massive explosion rocked the sea. The ship split in two and sunk in less than a minute.

Ships from the *Juneau*'s squadron thought for sure no one had survived. In fact, more than one hundred sailors clung to three rafts and bits of wreckage in the sea. Like

Rickenbacker and the B-17 crew, the castaways were left without food or drinking water. They were tormented by sharks and helpless against the sun and the sea.

But there was nothing inspiring about the way this story ended. The navy knew where the survivors were. And yet, messages were lost in the confusion of battle. Even when it was clear what had happened, the navy delayed the rescue for fear the Japanese were still patrolling the area. Rescue planes finally arrived six days after the battle. Only ten men were still alive. The rest had died from their wounds, from thirst, or from shark attacks.

———◆———

By the time Rickenbacker got back to Samoa, Adamson and Reynolds were ready to travel. The three of them flew back to the States, and the men went their separate ways.

Rickenbacker had a tearful reunion with Adelaide and their two sons, then went immediately to the Pentagon to report on his mission.

Cherry went to Washington, D.C., to help redesign the Air Force's survival equipment.

Whittaker went on tour telling his story to war workers on the Pacific coast.

Bartek went home to see his parents and embarked on a speaking tour of his own.

Homecoming: Eddie greets the public on his return to New York, with his wife, Adelaide, and New York City mayor Fiorello La Guardia.

Everywhere they traveled, the men were welcomed like heroes. When DeAngelis came home to Nesquehoning, Pennsylvania, there were 4,000 people in the streets to greet him—more than the entire population of the town. "I knew I had friends," he said, "but I didn't know I had this many."

Eddie, of course, got the biggest reception of all. A military band greeted him when he touched down in Washington, D.C. Once again, the newspapers hailed his "courage," his "daring," and his "determination."

The rest of the crew didn't feel as warm toward Rickenbacker. In public, they said all the right things. But they remembered the tirades and the power struggles they'd endured in the open ocean. A navigator on board the plane that flew them back to Hawaii overheard one of the men saying, "We stayed alive on that raft just to watch that son of a b_ _ _ _ get all the credit."

In fact, as the men told and retold the story of their ordeal, they all gave credit to a higher authority than Rickenbacker: God. They didn't have a lot to rely on out there besides Bartek's Bible and their own prayers. To most of the men, their survival began to seem like part of a divine plan.

For Whittaker it was a full-on conversion experience. In the bomber, before the ordeal, he had been scornful when DeAngelis wanted to pray. By the end, he was convinced that God had been watching over the rafts. He took the bird that landed on Rickenbacker's head as a sign that prayers get answered. When a rain squall appeared to travel against the wind to dump freshwater on them, it seemed like a miracle. He wrote a book about the ordeal, called *We Thought We Heard the Angels Sing.*

Like Whittaker, Bartek claimed he hadn't been especially religious as a kid. In January, two months after they were rescued, he told an audience of war workers that he wanted to become a minister. "After what happened to us out there . . . I feel I'm a true believer," he said.

One voice, of course, was absent from all the post-rescue storytelling. That was the voice of Alex Kaczmarczyk. History has left no record of his mother's beliefs. We know only that she hadn't heard about the rescue yet when the phone rang on November 14. There was a reporter on the line, calling to talk about her son's death. She burst into tears. "He was the only one . . . ," she cried, and hung up the phone.

In 1942, millions of people had to live with the news that someone close to them had been stolen away. In twenty-two days, seven men had survived on rafts in the Pacific. In that same twenty-two days, more than 2,000

Americans died in battle. On the USS *Juneau* alone, 90 men were left to die in the ocean while Rickenbacker and the B-17 crew drank soup and fruit juice on Funafuti. And the fighting stretched across the globe, from Guadalcanal to China to Eastern Europe to North Africa. On average, in every three-week period of the war, more than 500,000 people died. Each one of those deaths led to an announcement—a letter, a phone call, a knock at the door. And each announcement left a person at home to wonder why their son, their daughter, their husband had been killed while others survived.

At least some of those people read the *New York Times* on November 24, two weeks after the rescue of Rickenbacker and the crew. They might have seen a small article at the bottom of page 24 that puzzled over the meaning of the crew's survival: "We do not know why [Death] sometimes comes so close and then goes away. Often he takes the very bravest—this we know. He takes the generous, who give up their places in the lifeboat. He takes the compassionate, who will not let a wounded man suffer unaided between the lines. He takes those who love liberty so much that they will not bow to the oppressor.

"We shall never pierce this mystery," the article went on. "We can only rejoice that brave men sometimes come safely home from desperate peril."

Safe at Last: Bartek, Cherry, DeAngelis, and Whittaker (with the crew members of a Catalina seaplane) are all smiles, reunited after their rescue.

GLOSSARY

altimeter: a tool that measures how high something—such as an airplane—is off the ground

bulkhead: a wall that separates two different compartments in a ship or a plane

ditch: to make an emergency landing in water

fuselage: the main body of an airplane, where the passengers, crew, and cargo are carried

hangar: a large, typically enclosed building used to store aircraft

leave: a vacation, for military personnel

leeward: the side that's sheltered from the wind

magazine: a room or compartment where ammunition and explosives are stored

octant: a device you can use to determine your position by measuring your relationship to the sun or the stars

Pygmy: name for a person of an ethnic group whose members are unusually short

raise: to connect with someone by radio

Zero: model name of a famous, highly maneuverable fighter plane used by the Japanese during World War II

AUTHOR'S NOTE

In some ways, this story was easy to retell because nearly everyone, at the time, had something to say about it. Rickenbacker isn't exactly a household name now, but ask your grandfather about him and he'll probably say something like, "Eddie? Sure, I remember him."

When the B-17 crew came back to the States, the men were in high demand. Newspaper reporters mobbed them. Editors were desperate for a hopeful story to run next to all the frightening news from around the globe.

Because everyone wanted to hear the story, there are plenty of sources available now. In addition to the newspaper accounts, three of the men were interviewed at length for a feature film about Rickenbacker's life. Four of them wrote books with varying degrees of help from ghost writers.

I decided not to quote or refer to any of the accounts directly. Survival stories are driven by suspense—who's going to make it and who is not? Once you know that someone wrote about his ordeal after the fact, you have the answer. Instead I used the accounts to reconstruct what happened, and to try to get inside each man's thoughts and feelings while he was stranded on the rafts.

I did include conversations that the men remember having taken place during the ordeal. Read them the way you should read most dialogue in nonfiction—as an educated reconstruction. Only in rare cases—say, a space flight recorded by NASA—does a historian have a word-for-word transcription of what people actually said. Otherwise, you have only memory, which tends to make everyone wittier and more eloquent as time goes on. I stuck to conversations that either were echoed closely in more than one source or rang true to me, given what I had learned about each man in my research for this book.

The five men who left detailed accounts behind— Rickenbacker, Whittaker, Bartek, Adamson, and DeAngelis—each had slightly different stories to tell. They disagreed about when things happened and how. They had varying opinions of one another and especially of Rickenbacker. To write nonfiction is to dig through the contradictions and tell the story you think is closest to the truth.

Most of the factual discrepancies were small. Did the bird land on Rickenbacker's head on the sixth day, the seventh, or the eighth? Did Rickenbacker carve up the oranges, or did Adamson? When I couldn't answer those questions, I left my account vague. But often I felt confident making a call based on the evidence. I gave more credibility to the accounts that were written within months after the rescue: Rickenbacker's, Whittaker's, and Bartek's. Adamson wrote his four years later in an adoring biography of Rickenbacker, and he's noticeably less specific about the day-to-day details of the ordeal. The mental state of the author mattered to me, too. Whittaker and Rickenbacker were in the best shape in the rafts, and it shows in the sharpness of their accounts. In many cases, logic dictated my narrative choices. By the middle of the first week, for instance, Adamson's back was in such bad shape that he couldn't pull a magazine out of his pocket. I don't think he was the one chosen to carve oranges and fish into precisely equal pieces for eight starving men.

The toughest issue to sort out was Rickenbacker's relationship with the rest of the men on the rafts. Rickenbacker himself doesn't downplay how harshly he treated his raft mates. But it's all part of a portrait of himself as a can-do man of action who saved his comrades by driving them mercilessly to keep their spirits up. That may be close to the truth. People who study the survivors of long ordeals say that it helps tremendously to have one person who takes charge and gives the group a clear direction. But was it really a strategy on Rickenbacker's part? Or was he just a hot-tempered old crank who couldn't stand it when men didn't live up to his tough-guy ideal?

In public, the crew pretty much stuck to Rickenbacker's version of the story. It was wartime, after all; they were soldiers, and Rickenbacker was a national hero. But when Bartek and DeAngelis were interviewed by the film producers, you can hear them let their guard down. Bartek says Rickenbacker barely did any work himself; instead he ordered Bartek to do all the bailing and the pumping. Both Bartek and DeAngelis are ambivalent about whether Rickenbacker really helped them survive. Fifty years later, in another interview, Bartek said the entire crew blamed Rickenbacker for putting them in danger in the first place. According to Rickenbacker's biographer, W. David Lewis, Cherry refused to talk about Rickenbacker for the rest of his life.

I hope this extra background helps to explain why I find this story so interesting. It's a great, nail-biting tale of survival. But it's also a behind-the-scenes look at how heroes are made. Do we want to believe that six people survived because they had Eddie Rickenbacker on board? Or were they just lucky not to have gone into the ordeal in a weakened state like Alex? Do hunger, thirst, and desperation really lead to great acts of heroism? Or do they expose us for what we really are—simply human?

SOURCES

First-Person Accounts
The ordeal as told by the men who were on the rafts.

Adamson, Hans Christian. *Eddie Rickenbacker.* New York: Macmillan, 1946.

Bartek, Johnny. *Life Out There: A Story of Faith and Courage.* New York: Charles Scribner's Sons, 1943.

———. Interview with David Lewis and Dwayne Cox, Nov. 20, 1998. Auburn University Special Collections.

———. Speech About the Rickenbacker Rescue, Nov. 19, 1998. Auburn University Special Collections.

———. Interview with representatives of Twentieth Century Fox Film Company, July 21, 1943. Auburn University Special Collections.

DeAngelis, John J. Interview with representatives of Twentieth Century Fox Film Company, July 8, 1943. Auburn University Special Collections.

Rickenbacker, Edward V. *Seven Came Through*. New York: Doubleday, Doran and Company, 1943.

———. "Pacific Mission: As Related by Captain Edward V. Rickenbacker." Statement prepared for Eureka Pictures, December 1942.

———. *Rickenbacker: An Autobiography*. Englewood Cliffs, NJ: Prentice-Hall, 1967.

United States Marine Corps. "Report of Rescue of Captain Rickenbacker and Party, 11–12 November, 1942," Nov. 15, 1942. Auburn University Special Collections.

Whittaker, James C. *We Thought We Heard the Angels Sing*. New York: E.P. Dutton, 1943.

Background

Books that helped me understand the physiology and psychology of survival, the war going on around the B-17 crew, and more.

Allen, Thomas B. *Shark Attacks: Their Causes and Avoidance.* Guilford, CT: Lyons Press, 2001.

Bennet, Glin. *Beyond Endurance: Survival at the Extremes.* New York: St. Martin's/Mare, 1983.

Frank, Richard B. *Guadalcanal: The Definitive Account of the Landmark Battle.* New York: Penguin, 1990.

Gonzales, Laurence. *Deep Survival: Who Lives, Who Dies, and Why.* New York: W.W. Norton, 2003.

Kurzman, Dan. *Left to Die: The Tragedy of the USS Juneau.* New York: Simon & Schuster, 1994.

Leach, John. *Survival Psychology.* London: Palgrave Macmillan, 1994.

Leckie, Robert. *Challenge for the Pacific: Guadalcanal: The Turning Point of the War.* New York: Bantam Books, 2010.

Leslie, Edward E. *Desperate Journeys, Abandoned Souls: True Stories of Castaways and Other Survivors.* Boston: Houghton Mifflin, 1988.

Lewis, W. David. *Eddie Rickenbacker: An American Hero in the Twentieth Century.* Baltimore: Johns Hopkins University Press, 2005.

Philbrick, Nathaniel. *In the Heart of the Sea: The Tragedy of the Whaleship* Essex. New York: Penguin, 2000.

Ross, John F. *Enduring Courage: Ace Pilot Eddie Rickenbacker and the Dawn of the Age of Speed.* New York: St. Martin's Press, 2014.

Toll, Ian W. *Pacific Crucible: War at Sea in the Pacific, 1941–1942.* New York: W.W. Norton, 2012.

Trumbull, Robert. *The Raft.* Annapolis, MD: Naval Institute Press, 1942.

Newspapers and Magazines

Thanks in part to Rickenbacker, who kept scrapbooks documenting his life in detail, it's not difficult to follow coverage of the ordeal day-by-day in the press. There were too many articles written to list them all here, but many are cited throughout the book.

ACKNOWLEDGMENTS

This project would have been lost from the start without support from a lot of people. Jim Nolte and Taylor Davis-Van Atta at the Vermont College of the Fine Arts Library unearthed books from around the country. John Varner at Auburn University Archives sent stacks of photocopies of transcripts and scrapbooks from their exhaustive collection of Rickenbacker's papers. At a time when you can no longer hold most correspondence in your hand, it was weirdly comforting to sit in my chair, weighted down by several pounds of paper.

Thanks to Laura Williams McCaffrey, Leda Schubert, and Daphne Kalmar, who are indispensible after-work confidantes for someone who works alone all day. I am particularly indebted to Laura, who has read pages wisely and warmly for more years than I can count.

Thanks to Vermont College of the Fine Arts for helping to give me the tools and the attitude of a writer—and especially to Tobin Anderson for sharing his genius with me as a teacher. Marc Aronson and John Glenn have given me a lot during years of collaboration, and thanks are due to Marc for the series title. Lauren Tarshis has modeled how to edit, write, and live all at once—and tell a mighty fine survival story at the same time. Elizabeth Ward has taught me more, and put up with me longer, than anyone.

Paige Hazzan at Scholastic believed in the idea for this series and devoted her time and expert eye to the text. Miriam Altshuler has been all one can ask for in an agent—tough and caring, pragmatic and humane.

Thanks, finally, to Jill for giving me the space, the time, and the encouragement to write; to Zoë and Finn for being exactly who they are; and to Richard Olson and Estie Lawrence, who surrounded me with books from the time I could walk.

ABOUT THE AUTHOR

TOD OLSON is the author of the historical fiction series *How to Get Rich*. He works as an editor, holds an MFA from Vermont College of the Fine Arts, and lives in Vermont with his family, his mountain bike, and his electric reclining chair.